Georgia
US History EOC

SUCCESS STRATEGIES

**Georgia EOC Test Review
for the Georgia End of
Course Tests**

Need more help? Check out our flashcards at: http://MometrixFlashcards.com/Georgia

TABLE OF CONTENTS

Top 15 Test Taking Tips

1. Know the test directions, duration, topics, question types, how many questions
2. Setup a flexible study schedule at least 3-4 weeks before test day
3. Study during the time of day you are most alert, relaxed, and stress free
4. Maximize your learning style; visual learner use visual study aids, auditory learner use auditory study aids
5. Focus on your weakest knowledge base
6. Find a study partner to review with and help clarify questions
7. Practice, practice, practice
8. Get a good night's sleep; don't try to cram the night before the test
9. Eat a well balanced meal
10. Wear comfortable, loose fitting, layered clothing; prepare for it to be either cold or hot during the test
11. Eliminate the obviously wrong answer choices, then guess the first remaining choice
12. Pace yourself; don't rush, but keep working and move on if you get stuck
13. Maintain a positive attitude even if the test is going poorly
14. Keep your first answer unless you are positive it is wrong
15. Check your work, don't make a careless mistake

Colonization through the Constitution

North America

Basic geography
North America is the third largest continent in the world. It includes all the mainland of the northern landmass in the western hemisphere, as well as all the related offshore islands that lie north of the Isthmus of Panama. People often will call Canada and the United States "Anglo-America," and Mexico, Central America, and the Caribbean "Middle America." North America is bounded on the north by the Arctic Ocean, on the west by the Pacific Ocean and the Bering Sea, and on the east by the Atlantic Ocean and the Gulf of Mexico. The Gulf of Mexico is the largest body of water to indent the coast, the second-largest being the Hudson Bay. The Gulf of St. Lawrence and the Gulf of California also indent the coast of North America severely. There are a number of large islands off the coast of North America: Greenland, the Arctic Archipelago, the Greater and Lesser Antilles, the Alexander Archipelago, and the Aleutian Islands. The highest point in North America is Mt. McKinley, Alaska, and the lowest point is in Death Valley. The Missouri-Mississippi River System is the longest in North America; it is also the world's largest inland waterway system. Ships are able to enter the heart of the North America by means of the Saint Lawrence Seaway. Other major rivers of the North American continent are the Colorado, Mackenzie, Nelson, Rio Grande, St. Lawrence, Susquehanna, Columbia, and Yukon.

Physiography
North America can be divided into five regions. The Canadian Shield is an area of stable, ancient rock that occupies the northeast corner of the continent, including Greenland. The Appalachian Mountains are an old and worn-down mountain system extending from the Gaspe Peninsula to Alabama. The Atlantic-Gulf Coastal Plain is a stretch of lowlands running from New England to Mexico. The Interior Lowlands extend from central Canada to the Gulf Coast. The North American Cordillera is a mountain system that includes both the Pacific Margin and the Rocky Mountains. Another lesser formation, the Transverse Volcanic Range, extends below Mexico City.

Climate
The continent of North America contains every climatic zone, ranging from the tropical rain forests and savannas in the lowlands of Central America to the permanent ice caps in the middle of Greenland. In northern Canada, the climate is mostly subarctic and tundra. These are also found in northern Alaska. The two major mountain ranges of the continent affect the climate greatly. In the interior regions close to the Appalachian and Rocky Mountains, the climate and terrain is mostly semiarid and desert. These areas are largely prevented from receiving westerly winds and storms. Most of North America, however, has a temperate climate and is hospitable to settlement and agriculture.

Native Americans

Native Americans of the Plains area
The Plains area extends from barely north of the Canadian border to Texas. Before the arrival of Columbus, the tribes in this region were either nomadic or sedentary. The sedentary tribes settled in the great river valleys and grew corn, squash, and beans. The

- 2 -

nomads, meanwhile, moved their goods around on sleds pulled by dogs. They hunted buffalo by driving them into enclosures or by herding them with fires. There was also a fair amount of trade with the sedentary tribes. Many Native American tribes migrated into the Plains region; among them were the Sioux, Comanche, Kiowa, Navajo, and Apache. The tribes were typically governed by a chief, who would eventually be supplanted in a violent coup.

Native Americans of the Northwest Coast area

The main Native American tribes in the Northwest Coast are the Kwakiutl, Haida, and Nootka. These people lived in a densely forested area, with a temperate climate and heavy rainfall, and they survived mainly on salmon. The Native Americans in this region built their houses out of wood, and made canoes from cedar. These tribes built totem poles in their permanent winter villages which were elaborately carved with the faces of the tribal animal gods. They had a strict social hierarchy, with chiefs, nobles, commoners, and slaves. The Native Americans of the Pacific Northwest would be largely untouched by Europeans until the 18th century, when fur trappers began to encroach upon their territory.

Native Americans of the Eastern Woodlands

The Eastern Woodlands extend from the Mississippi River east to the Atlantic Ocean. The tribes of this region included the Natchez, Choctaw, Cherokee, and Creek. The people of the northeast region mostly farmed and hunted deer. They used canoes made of birch bark. The people in the Iroquois family of tribes lived either in dome-shaped wigwams or in long houses, and would typically wear clothing made from the skin of deer, often painting their faces. In the southern part of the Eastern Woodlands, there were semi-nomadic tribes who survived by hunting, fishing, and gathering. These people hunted with a bow and arrow or with a blowgun. They developed highly detailed pottery and surrounded their villages with elaborate defenses.

Native Americans of the Plateau area

The Plateau area runs from just above the Canadian border into the American southwest. Some of the larger tribes in the region were the Spokane, Nez Perce, and Shoshone. The area where these tribes dwelled was not especially hospitable, so they spent much of their time trying to eke out a living. The tribes in the south gathered fruits and nuts, and hunted small animals. The tribes in the north fished for salmon and gathered roots and berries. Later on, these tribes would begin to hunt buffalo. Many of the northern tribes had permanent winter villages, most of which were along waterways. They borrowed the architecture of the tepee from the Plains Indians, though some tribes had long houses covered with bark.

Native Americans of the Southwest area

The Southwest area extends across Arizona, New Mexico, Colorado, and Utah. A seminomadic people known as the Basket Makers hunted with the atlatl, a device that made it possible to throw a spear accurately over a great distance. The tribes in this area lived in pit dwellings which were partly underground. Later, ancestors of the Pueblo Indians would develop community houses set into the side of cliffs and canyons. These cliff dwellings often had a ceremonial fire pit, or kiva. These people grew corn, beans, squash, cotton, and tobacco, they killed rabbits with a wooden stick, and they traded their textiles to nomadic tribes for buffalo meat. The tribes of the Southwest also had a complex mythology and religious system.

Native Americans of the region now known as Canada
The Native Americans that inhabited the region now known as Canada included the Chippewa. This region was not especially hospitable to life and therefore there was little farming. Instead, the tribes hunted, gathered, fished, and trapped in order to survive. There were many groups of nomadic hunters who moved around from season to season. Caribou was the most popular game, and people would make all kinds of products out of parts of the animal, including caribou shoes, caribou nets, and caribou bags. These people relied on snowshoes to allow them to move quickly and without falling into icy lakes. Many of the tribes in this region had a shaman, a mystic who provided spiritual guidance to the members of the tribe.

English interest in the New World

The English lagged somewhat behind other European nations in exploration of the New World. Finally, however, a combination of economic and social incentives convinced them to look west. For one thing, the enclosure movement in England had made land very scarce, and the practice of primogeniture meant that only the eldest son could inherit the land. For these reasons, many Englishmen moved to the New World for the promise of cheap land. England also had a large population at this time and thus the government viewed the New World as a good place to send criminals and beggars. Another reason for the increase in interest in America was the Protestant Reformation. Many English Catholics and Protestants felt alienated by the new Church of England, and wanted to find somewhere in which they could worship more freely.

First European explorers in America

Although Christopher Columbus frequently gets credit for "discovering" America (notwithstanding the fact that people were already living on the continent), Vikings from Scandinavia actually arrived in about A.D. 1000. These explorers constructed no permanent settlements, however, and did not remain for long. It was not until economic expansion in Europe made exploration worthwhile that explorers would return. Columbus, and the explorers who would come later, were looking for the Northwest Passage that would take them directly to Asia and were actually annoyed by the new land that kept getting in the way. Columbus actually died believing that he had landed in some outpost of India (hence, "Indians").

Settling of North America by the English

The first English attempt to found a colony in the New World was made by Sir Humphrey Gilbert in Newfoundland in 1583, and was a complete failure. Sir Walter Raleigh would lead two more failed attempts at founding a colony on Roanoke Island in 1586 and 1588. The second of these colonies is known as the Lost Colony, because it disappeared without a trace while Raleigh was gone. Finally, the British were able to establish a permanent colony at Jamestown, Virginia in 1607. The settlers in Jamestown came for gold and to convert the Natives to Christianity. One of the important events of the early years of Jamestown was the issuing of the Virginia Charter, which declared that English settlers in the New World would be treated as Englishmen with full English rights.

- 4 -

Beginnings of the Virginia colony
The English colony of Virginia, which began at Jamestown, was at first plagued by a poor location and a paucity of skilled laborers. Captain John Smith was elected leader in 1608, and he proved to be the strict leader the colony needed to survive. A large proportion of the settlers would die during the winter of 1609-10. What finally saved the Virginia colony was the wild popularity of tobacco. In 1619, the House of Burgesses met, becoming the first legislative body to be formed in the New World. King James I of England correctly predicted that this would only lead to trouble for his nation. Also in 1619, 20 African indentured servants arrived on a Dutch warship; Virginia would become the first colony to legalize slavery, in 1660.

Virginia officially became a Royal Colony in 1624. This was in part because the Virginia Company (the joint-stock company that had previously administered affairs) had gone bankrupt, and partly because King James I wanted to exercise more control. After the English Civil War of the 1640s, many of the supporters of the king, known as cavaliers, settled in Virginia. During this period, the wealthy colonists began claiming the coastal land and pushing the poor people farther inland, where they were prey to Indian attacks and were underrepresented in the House of Burgesses. Frustrated, a group of settlers led by Nathaniel Bacon burned Jamestown to the ground. Bacon's Rebellion, as it came to be known, is thought of by some as a harbinger of things to come.

Beginnings of the colonies of Maryland, the Carolinas, and Georgia
Maryland was established in 1634 as a proprietary colony, meaning it was exclusively owned by one person. The owner, Lord Baltimore, ran his colony like a feudal estate. Maryland prospered because of tobacco and became a haven for persecuted Catholics. North Carolina was originally settled by Virginians, and quickly acquired a reputation as independent and democratic. Many English colonists avoided North Carolina because they felt it was overrun by pirates. South Carolina, meanwhile, was a proprietary colony established in 1670. South Carolina hosted a large number of religious groups. Georgia, meanwhile, was a proprietary colony established in 1733. Its namesake, George II, hoped that it would be a buffer zone between the colonists and the Indians, and populated it almost exclusively with criminals and debtors.

Southern colonies

Social life in the Southern colonies
The social lives of the Southern colonists were filled with dancing, card-playing, cotillions, hunts, and large community dinners. Southerners were considered to be very optimistic in temperament, in contrast to their more dour Northern counterparts. It was extremely difficult to move up in the social hierarchy in the South; the richer colonists generally took the best land and thus were able to maintain their position in the economy and in the government, as the poor had to move away from the towns to find farmland. Because farming was the only available occupation, there were not any venues for ambitious men to distinguish themselves. North Carolina was generally considered to be the state with the least social stratification.

Economic life in the Southern colonies
In the early days of the Southern colonies, most people lived on small farms. Although they made up a tiny part of the population, the owners of the coastal plantations wielded enormous power. These aristocrats typically grew a single crop on their lands: in North

Carolina, Virginia, and Maryland, tobacco was the cash crop, while the large growers in South Carolina and Georgia favored rice and indigo. Plantations, like the feudal manors of the past, were almost totally self-sufficient units, although the owners imported most of their luxury items from England. The Southern colonies had the closest ties with England, mainly because England provided the market for their tobacco; crops grown in the colonies were sold back in England by agents (known as factors).

Religious and political life in the Southern colonies
In all of the Southern colonies, the Anglican Church was supported by taxes. Anyone who wanted to enter politics would have to be a member of the Church, though the majority of the colonists were not. In general, the Southern colonies had the greatest degree of religious toleration. Politics during this period were largely controlled by the planter aristocracy. Each Southern colony had a governor (chosen by the colony's English sponsor), a governor's council, and an assembly to represent the people. During the 1700s, these assemblies took more and more power away from the governors. In order to run for office, a man had to be a member of the Anglican Church; many people, including Thomas Jefferson, would acquire membership in the Church and then never set foot inside it again.

Life expectancy and education in the Southern colonies
The average man in the Southern colonies could expect to live 35 years. This was in part due to disease; stagnant water and unfamiliar heat helped the spread of many contagions throughout the population, and malaria was a constant danger. Because of the high mortality rate, most families were very large. Also, education was not a high priority in the colonies in those days. One problem was that the population was too scattered for a central public school to be possible. Wealthy plantation owners would hire a tutor for their children, who might later be sent off to William and Mary or one of the new schools up North: Harvard, Yale, or Princeton. For the less affluent, however, it was more likely that any education would be received as an apprentice of an experienced craftsman.

Slavery legalized in the Southern colonies
Between 1640 and 1660, the Southern colonies slowly evolved from a system of servitude to one of slavery. In 1661, Virginia became the first colony to legalize chattel slavery for life, and made it such that the children of slaves would be slaves as well. The number of slaves increased dramatically in the 1680s after the Royal African Company lost its monopoly and the industry was thrown open to anyone. Virginia established slave codes to keep revolts down: slaves could not be taught to read, could not gather together, could not have weapons, and could not leave the plantation without written permission. Naturally, slaves often rebelled against their treatment, but they were outnumbered and overpowered.

Beginning of the slave trade in the Southern colonies
After periods in which Native Americans or indentured servants from England were used as laborers, most of the labor in the Southern British North American colonies was performed by African slaves. These slaves were taken in wars between African chieftains, and then sold to European traders. Oftentimes, the African leaders would trade slaves for guns in order to protect themselves from other slave traders. Several African states, most notably the Yoruba and the Dahomey, became wealthy from this trade. The journey from West Africa to the West Indies was dangerous and depressing, and many slaves died en route. Before they were sold into the American colonies, slaves first worked in the brutal heat of the sugar plantations of the British West Indies. Only about half would survive long enough to see America.

Early resistance to slavery
Many slaves resisted submission, and many died as a result. For any serious offense, a slave would be executed in front of his or her peers as a deterrent. From its inception, there was resistance to slavery. In 1688, the Quakers declared that slavery was inhuman and a violation of the Bible. Many felt that slavery degraded both master and slave. In order to justify the hateful institution, slave-owners declared that blacks were less than human, or that, as descendants of the Biblical figure Ham, they were ordered by God to serve whites. The hymn "Amazing Grace" was written by guilt-wracked former slave trader John Newton. Slaves could only become free by proving mulatto (half white) status, or by buying their freedom (some masters would allow their slaves to work for pay on the weekends).

Massachusetts colony

Puritanism and the Pilgrims in Massachusetts colony
Puritans believe in the idea of predestination, meaning that God has already chosen which people will get into heaven. In order to suggest to others (and to themselves) that they were among the elect, Puritans were obsessed with maintaining proper decorum in public. Those Puritans who wanted to fully separate from the Church of England were known as Pilgrims (or Separatists). The Pilgrims originally went to Holland, but after determining that they would be unable to make a good life there, they got permission from the Virginia Company to settle in the northern part of the Virginia colony in 1620. The Plymouth Company was commissioned, and the Mayflower set sail. Because of storms and poor navigation, however, they ended up in the area that would come to be known as Massachusetts. One of the early moves of the group was to agree to the Mayflower Compact, whereby all members of the group would be bound to the will of the majority.

Political and social life in the early Massachusetts colonies
The Massachusetts Bay Puritans were known for religious intolerance and a general suspicion of democracy. Even though they had left England because of religious persecution, they did not set up their colony as a safe haven for others. One of the people who was kicked out of the colony for blasphemy was Roger Williams, who went on to found a colony at Providence. Williams taught that the colonists should be fair to the Indians, and that political leaders should stay out of religion. Roger Williams eventually founded the Baptist Church. The Puritans generally felt that the common people were incapable of governing themselves and should be looked after by their government. Also, many Puritans objected to democracy because they felt it was inefficient.

Puritans in the Massachusetts colony
The Puritans established the colony of Massachusetts Bay in 1630. They hoped to purify the Church of England and then return to Europe with a new and improved religion. The Massachusetts Bay Puritans were more immediately successful than other fledgling colonies because they brought enough supplies, arrived in the springtime, and had good leadership (including John Winthrop). Puritans fished, cut timber for ships, and trapped fur. The local government was inextricably bound with the church; only church members were allowed to vote for the General Court (similar to the House of Burgesses), although everyone was required to pay taxes. The Puritans established a Bible Commonwealth that would last 50 years. During this time, Old Testament law was the law of the community.

Dominion of New England

The impertinence of the Massachusetts Bay colony was a constant annoyance to King Charles II and he thus punished them by granting charters to rival colonies in Connecticut and Rhode Island and by creating the Dominion of New England. The purpose of this organization was to boost trade by enforcing the Navigation Acts of 1660 and 1663, which stated that all trade had to be done on English ships and had to pass through England before it could go anywhere else. The English, of course, made the colonists pay a tax on any exports that were not bound for England. The colonists loathed the Dominion government, not only because of its economic penalties, but because it tried to promote the Anglican Church in America. A rebellion against the Dominion probably would have occurred if the Glorious Revolution in England had not ended it prematurely.

English Civil War and the New England Confederation

During the English Civil War, the Puritans tried to separate from the Church of England; they issued the Body of Liberties, which stated that the Massachusetts Bay was independent of England and was therefore no longer bound by English Civil Law, that there could be no arbitrary governors appointed to dissolve a local legislature, and that town meetings of qualified voters would be held to discuss local issues. Later, in 1643, a New England Confederation was formed, consisting of Massachusetts Bay, New Plymouth, Connecticut River Valley, and New Haven. The goals of this confederation were to protect the colonists from the French (in Canada) and the Indians; to safeguard their commercial interests from the Dutch in New Netherlands (later New York); and to return runaway slaves.

Puritans

Social and religious life of the Puritans
There was more chance for social mobility in Massachusetts than in any other colony in America. This was mainly due to the diverse economy. As for religion, it dominated every area of an individual's life. The Puritan Church was known as the Congregational Church; at first, this was an exclusive group, but it gradually became easier to become a member. Indeed, by the mid-1600s religious fervor seemed to be waning in Massachusetts. A group called the Jeremiads warned the people that they were in danger of lapsing into atheism, but many people did not mind. Around this time, ministers began to offer half-way covenants, which gave church members partial privileges.

Land, demography, climate, economics, and slavery in Puritan life
The land settled by the Puritans was rocky and bare, and it took tremendous labor to subsist off of its products. Massachusetts had an extremely homogenous population, mainly because there was little reason to stay there other than to be among people of the same faith. Non-Puritan immigrants usually moved south, where the soil was better and the population was more tolerant. Because agriculture was so tricky, a more diverse economy developed in New England than existed in the South. Puritans engaged in fishing and trapping, and there were a number of craftsmen in each town. There were slaves in New England, though not nearly as many as in the South. Furthermore, slaves in New England were more commonly used as household servants than hard laborers.

Great Awakening

The Great Awakening was a religious revival in New England in the 1730s and 40s. It began in response to the growing secularism and was aided by the recent migrations into the cities, where it was easier for large crowds to form. Jonathan Edwards was one of the most famous preachers of this time. The Great Awakening was the first mass movement in America; it helped break down the divides between the various regions of the British colonies and led to the formation of some new Protestant denominations. Though the Revivalists did not directly advocate the abolition of slavery, they did suggest that there was divinity in all creation, and that therefore blacks were worthy of being converted to Christianity.

Salem Witch Trials

During the 1690s in New England, there was still a strong belief in Christian mysticism. Many people were paranoid about spiritualists and mediums. This, combined with perhaps some local feuds, led to 19 women and one man being executed for witchcraft in 1692. Most likely, however, the accused individuals were only suffering from delusions caused by a kind of hallucinogenic bread mold (ergot). The witch trials only stopped when people in high places began being accused. The Salem witch trials tarnished the image of the clergy for a long time, and further contributed to a general relaxation of religious fervor in this period.

New Netherlands colony

The Dutch East India Company hired the English explorer Henry Hudson to search for the Northwest Passage to Asia. Instead, he journeyed up the Hudson River and claimed the area now known as New York for the Dutch. The Dutch purchased Manhattan Island from the Manhattan Indians for $24, and established a town called New Amsterdam there, an aristocratic town, in which everyone had to be a member of the Dutch Reform Church. Eventually, in 1664, this Dutch settlement would be overwhelmed by the British colonies surrounding it. King Charles II gave the area to his successor, James, Duke of York, who quickly gave the town and colony the name it bears today.

Bible Commonwealth

The New England colonies started out as Bible Commonwealths, where Biblical law was local law, and a man's standing in the church determined his political power. Over time, however, New England became more liberal, and politics came to be dominated by the wealthy men rather than by the church leaders. Life expectancy in the New England colonies became roughly what it is today. Education was valued greatly in New England, and the fact that most people lived close to a town made it possible for more people to receive an inexpensive training. Puritans believed that ignorance of God's word could lead one to be tricked by the devil, and thus they made sure that all of their children learned to read.

Middle Colonies

Economic life, slavery, and society in the Middle Colonies
The Middle Colonies (New York, Pennsylvania, Delaware, East and West New Jersey) shared characteristics with both New England and the Southern colonies. The economy was diverse, though less so than in New England. Shipping and commerce would gradually become crucial in the port cities of Philadelphia and New York. There were plenty of slaves in the Middle Colonies, most of whom served as laborers on ships. The Dutch treated their slaves well; the English did not. People in these colonies tended to have a healthier lifestyle than their neighbors to the south, and therefore they tended to live longer. The diverse economy made social mobility possible, though large landowners were for the most part entrenched in positions of power.

Education, religion, and politics in the Middle Colonies
Most education in the Middle Colonies was received as an apprentice to a successful craftsman. Often, local churches would maintain schools during the week. The two main religious organizations in this region were the Anglican Church and the Dutch Reform Church, often at each other's throat because they were competing for members and tax dollars. A typical government in the Middle Colonies had a governor, a governor's council, and a representative assembly. Men were only allowed to vote if they owned property. The Middle Colonies had the most diverse population, mainly because they had available land and promised religious freedom (at least in Pennsylvania).

Pennsylvania colony

The Pennsylvania (literally "Penn's woods") was established by William Penn in 1681. Penn declared that the colony would provide religious and political freedom for all. The main religious group to settle in the area was the Society of Friends (Quakers). Quakers believed that every person could communicate with the divine, that the church should not be supported by tax dollars, and that all men are equal. The Quakers have always been pacifists, and they were the first group to oppose slavery. In Pennsylvania, voting rights were extended only to land holders or large taxpayers. The Charter of Liberties (1701) established a unicameral legislature working alongside a governor.

George Grenville

George Grenville became the prime minister of Britain in 1763, and immediately abandoned the policy of "salutary neglect" that had been upheld by Walpole. On the contrary, he asserted that the American colonists should have to pay for British military protection, even though the Americans claimed not to need it. According to the Proclamation of 1763, all American colonists were to stay east of the Appalachian Mountains. This policy was ostensibly created in order to protect the colonists in the wake of Chief Pontiac's Rebellion in 1763, in which Indians attacked colonists and were subsequently slaughtered by the British. Many colonists, however, felt that the Proclamation was a transparent attempt to maintain British control of the fur trade.

Stamp Act of 1765

The Stamp Act of 1765 was levied without the consent of the colonists. It specified that a stamp must be applied to all legal documents (there was considerable debate over the definition of this phrase) indicating that a tax had been paid for the defense of the colonies. This act was extremely unpopular, perhaps most because its presence was so visible; its implementation generated loud cries of "taxation without representation." The British responded by claiming that the colonists had "virtual representation" by members of Parliament. The colonists continued to claim that they needed direct and actual representation, although many feared that even if they were to get it, they would probably lose most votes anyway.

Sugar (Revenue) Act, Currency Act, and the Quartering Act

The *Sugar (Revenue) Act of 1764* established a duty on basically any products that were not British in origin: for instance molasses, indigo, and sugar. Unlike the Molasses Act, the Sugar Act was fully enforced. Most colonists resented this taxation, which they felt was used to fund the French and Indian War. The *Currency Act of 1764* forbade colonists from issuing paper money, and stated that all taxes paid to England must be paid in gold and silver rather than paper. This act eliminated the worthless Continental Dollar. The *Quartering Act of 1765* required colonists to provide bedding and food to the regiments of British soldiers in America. This regulation increased paranoia amongst the colonists, who began to wonder exactly why the British soldiers were there in the first place.

Townshend Acts

The *Townshend Acts*, named after Charles "Champagne Charlie" Townshend, the prime minister of Britain from 1766-1772, placed an indirect tax on household items coming into the colonies, and tightened the custom duties. The Acts also called for stricter vice-admiralty courts and established the Writs of Assistance, which were essentially blank search warrants. The colonists' response to the Townshend Acts was twofold: a pamphlet war was waged by men like John Dickinson, James Otis, and Samuel Adams; and there were also more violent protests, as for instance the Boston Massacre, in which a mob in the Boston Commons was fired on by the British, perhaps accidentally. Colonists used the "Massacre" as a rallying cry, and the Townshend Acts were repealed (with the notable exception of the tax on tea).

Stamp Act Congress, the Sons of Liberty and the Declaratory Act

The colonists created the *Stamp Act Congress* in Philadelphia in order to peacefully resolve the conflicts created by the Stamp Act. This group established the Non-importation Agreements, which amounted to a boycott of English products. At the same time, the *Sons of Liberty* in Boston were running amok: vandalizing British goods, tarring and feathering stamp collectors, and erecting so-called "liberty poles," from which collectors would be hung by their pants. In 1766, the new British prime minister Rockingham repealed the Stamp Act because the boycotts were damaging the British economy. In part to punish the colonists for their insubordination, in 1766 the British Parliament issued the *Declaratory Act*, which asserted that they had the right to legislate on behalf of the colonists at any time.

Tea Act of 1773 and the Boston Tea Party

The Tea Act was established by the British Parliament to aid the foundering British East India Company. The tax on tea established by the Townshend Acts had remained in effect even after the rest of the Acts were repealed, and the colonial boycott on British tea in

- 11 -

response was a major problem for the British East India Company. The Tea Act, therefore, created a governmental loan so that the Company could buy ships, and forced the colonists to buy the taxed tea. The colonists did not appreciate this act, and at the so-called Boston Tea Party the Sons of Liberty dressed as Indians and threw 90,000 pounds of tea into the Boston Harbor. This act cost the colonists many friends in Britain, as it seemed to be inconsistent with their usual defense of property rights.

Lord North, the Gaspee, the Committees of Correspondence and John Wilkes

Lord North succeeded Townshend as British prime minister in 1772. In this year, the Sons of Liberty set fire to the Gaspee, a British revenue ship, off the coast of Rhode Island. The Sons of Liberty were driven to further violence by Massachusetts governor Tom Hutchinson's announcement that his salary would be paid by the British. The Committees of Correspondence were subsequently formed to organize the protest against the British, and to keep colonists informed on British matters. At around this time, the British MP John Wilkes became a folk hero in the colonies because of his impassioned speeches in defense of liberty. Although Wilkes never spoke directly on behalf of the colonists, he was jailed for his speeches.

First Continental Congress

The First Continental Congress was held September 5, 1774, and was attended by a representative of every colony except Georgia. This Congress issued the Suffolk Resolves, stating that they would give Boston aid in the form of food and clothing, but would not take up arms on behalf of Boston. The Continental Association, an agreement not to buy or sell English goods, was formed. A conservative named Joseph Galloway advocated the creation of a Council of All Colonies, a legislative body which would share power with Parliament. The Galloway Plan was nixed by Massachusetts, however, because that colony refused to share power with any British authority. Massachusetts at this time was in a highly volatile state.

Coercive (Intolerable) Acts

The Coercive Acts, known as the Intolerable Acts in America, were issued in response to the Boston Tea Party, and had several parts. The Boston Port Act closed the port down, supposedly until such time as the destroyed tea was paid for, although this never happened. The Massachusetts Government Act put the colony under martial law. A military governor, Thomas Gage, was placed in charge of the colony. The Administration of Justice Act required that all judges, soldiers, and tax agents be English, and that all crimes be tried in England. The New Quartering Act asserted that British soldiers were allowed to enter private homes and demand lodging. The Quebec Act of 1774 declared that everything west of the Appalachians was Quebec; although this was basically done so that Britain could govern more effectively, it caused speculation among the colonists that the British were going to sell America to the French.

Second Continental Congress

The Second Continental Congress was held May 10, 1775 in Philadelphia. George Washington became the commander of the Americans, mainly because it was felt that he would be able to bring the Southern colonies into the fold. This Congress also drew up the

Olive Branch petition, a peace offering made to the King of England. The Articles of Confederation were drawn up here; their emphasis on states' rights proved to be a poor setup for organizing a comprehensive military strategy. This Congress created the Committees of Safety, a system for training community militias. This Congress created a bureaucracy for the purpose of organizing a navy and raising money. Finally, it was here that the colonists formally declared independence.

Thomas Gage and Paul Revere

Thomas Gage, the military governor of Massachusetts, was under increasing duress at the beginning of 1775 and asked the British government for either 20,000 more troops or a repeal of the Coercive Acts. Instead, Britain sent 2,000 troops, which Gage used to collect guns, gunpowder, and shot. On April 18 of 1775, the British troops sailed across Boston Harbor toward the large stockpile at Concord. Paul Revere then took his famous ride to warn the other colonists about the approach of the British. Although Revere was captured, his ride was finished by Samuel Prescott and William Dawes. On the way to Concord, in Lexington, shots were fired and 8 colonial militiamen were killed. The British then moved on to Concord, where the real fighting began.

Declaration of Independence

The Declaration of Independence was proposed at the Second Continental Congress by Richard Henry Lee, and was composed by a committee of Franklin, Jefferson, John Adams, Robert Livingston, and Roger Sherman. The document has three parts: a preamble and reasons for separation; a theory of government; and a formal declaration of war. Jefferson attempted to have it include a condemnation of slavery, but was rebuffed. The Declaration had many aims: to enlist help from other British colonies; to create a cause for which to fight; to motivate reluctant colonists; to ensure that captured Americans would be treated as prisoners of war; and to establish an American theory of government. In fulfilling this last purpose, Jefferson borrowed heavily from Enlightenment thinkers like Montesquieu, Rousseau, and Locke, asserting famously that "all men are created equal."

Reasons for declaring independence
At the time that the Declaration of Independence was issued, many colonists were opposed to complete separation from England. Many of them still considered themselves Englishmen and were afraid to be branded as traitors. They also realized that they were in uncharted waters: no revolt had ever been successful in winning independence. Finally, many colonists feared that even if they were successful in winning independence, the result would be chaos in America. The minds of many of these reluctant colonists were changed, however, by the Battle of Bunker Hill, which was won by the British. After this battle, King George II declared that the colonists were in a state of rebellion. Furthermore, the British labeled the members of the Second Continental Congress as traitors and ignored the Olive Branch petition. Confused colonists were further flamed by the British use of Hessian mercenary soldiers. The writings of Thomas Paine also converted many colonists to the revolutionary cause.

Significance of the Declaration of Independence
The issuing of the Declaration of Independence had effects both on the Revolutionary War and on world history at large. As far as its immediate effects, it changed the war in America from a war for liberty to a war for independence, by rhetorically emancipating America

from Britain. It also opened a path for the French Revolution a few years later, one motivated by the principles expressed in the Declaration. Revolutions in South America, Africa, and Asia have also used the Declaration of Independence as inspiration. In the subsequent history of the United States, the document would be used by abolitionists as an argument against slavery, and by suffragists as an argument for the right of women to vote.

Saratoga Campaign

The British military plan during the early stages of the Revolutionary War was known as the Saratoga campaign (or the German Plan). It called for a three-pronged attack aimed at capturing New York and thus separating the Northeast from the Southern colonies. This plan broke down because of the following reasons: One of the generals, Howe, was supposed to go up the Hudson River to Albany, but instead decided to go after Philadelphia. Another general, Burgoyne, was able to conquer Fort Ticonderoga, but then languished without supplies for months, and eventually had to surrender to colonial troops. The third general, St. Ledger, made considerable progress across New York from Lake Ontario, but lost steam after a series of small battles.

Battle of Saratoga

The colonial General Gates defeated the British General Burgoyne at the Battle of Saratoga in 1777. This defeat confirmed the failure of the British Saratoga Campaign. More importantly, perhaps, it convinced the French that the Americans could win the war. The French then signed the Treaty of Alliance in 1778, which supplied the Americans with money, men, and ships. This treaty was in part negotiated by Benjamin Franklin. The French were not necessarily motivated by a spirit of goodwill towards the Americans; they hoped to gain back the territory they had lost in the French and Indian War. Moreover, the French believed that by aiding the Americans in the Revolutionary War they could position themselves to colonize parts of North America as yet unclaimed.

Southern Campaign in the Revolutionary War

The British military campaign in the Southern colonies was planned by Sir Henry Clinton and implemented by General Cornwallis in the years 1778 to 1781. Cornwallis quickly took Savannah and Charleston and then moved into the interior of South Carolina. Here and in North Carolina a series of bloody battles (many of them against the great American general Nathaniel Greene) weakened Cornwallis and forced him to make a supply run to Yorktown on the Virginia coast. There, the British suffered a naval defeat at the hands of the French, and then were routed by Washington-led troops. During their retreat, the British naval forces were further weakened by a violent storm, and Cornwallis was forced to surrender on October 17, 1781.

Articles of Confederation

The Articles of Confederation were largely ineffective because they gave too much power to the states and too little to a central government. Many historians now say that the best thing about the Articles were that they showed the authors of the Constitution what to avoid. Part of the Articles was the Land Ordinance of 1785, a plan created by Jefferson for dividing the Western land into organized townships. The sale of land in these territories helped generate money for the new government. The Northwest Ordinance of 1787 divided the land above the Ohio River into five territories, which would soon become states. This ordinance would become the model for how all future states would be formed.

Passing legislation under the Articles of Confederation
After the Revolutionary War, the United States found itself in a massive and troubling debt. Meanwhile, Congress was having great difficulty passing any legislation because in order to be made into law, a bill had to receive 9 of 13 votes, and there were often fewer than 10 representatives present. The government had no chief executive, and thus law enforcement was left to the states. Another major problem was that the lack of a central court system made it hard to resolve disputes between citizens from different states, or between the states themselves. Congress did not have the power to tax the people directly, and could only request funds. Furthermore, although Congress could issue currency, it had no authority to keep the states from issuing currency of their own, so wild inflation and depreciation were common.

Foreign Affairs under the Articles of Confederation
Both the Americans and the British violated the terms of the Treaty of Paris, which had ended the Revolutionary War in 1783. The British, for instance, never fully abandoned their lucrative fur trade in the Ohio Valley. Americans, on the other hand, never paid back their pre-war debts. Meanwhile, the Spanish (who controlled Louisiana and Florida) openly challenged American borders in the South, at times encouraging Native Americans to make war on the fledgling nation. Americans sought the right of deposit on the Mississippi; that is, the right to load material from a boat to a dock. The Spanish were not quick to grant this right. Meanwhile, American ships were forced to pay tribute to the Barbary states in order to trade in the Mediterranean.

Competing currencies and legislative troubles under the Articles of Confederation
Under the Articles of Confederation, Congress did not have the power to raise an army directly; it could only ask for troops from the states. The problems with this arrangement were amply demonstrated by Shay's Rebellion in Massachusetts in 1786 and 1787. This rebellion was in part a response to the economic uncertainty by competing currencies. Under the Articles, Congress did not have the power to regulate inter-state or foreign commerce. Each state in the confederation had different tariffs and trade regulations, and no foreign countries would enter into trade agreements with a nation so disorganized. In short, the Articles of Confederation left America unable to maintain order at home, unable to gain respect abroad, and unable to improve its economy.

Legacy of the Revolutionary War

After the conclusion of the Revolutionary War, neither the Proclamation of 1763 nor the Quebec Act applied, and thus colonists could move west across the Appalachians. A few British loyalists lost their land. After the war, many states moved to separate the church and state; in Virginia, for instance, Thomas Jefferson wrote the Virginia Statute of Religious Freedom, creating total separation in that state. States also revised the Criminal Codes, in an effort to make the punishment more closely fit the crime. Finally, whereas in 1750 most citizens did not question the institution of slavery, by 1780 many states began to examine this policy. Vermont was the first state to abolish slavery. Meanwhile, Southern states argued that the war would not have been won without slave labor.

Constitution

On September 17, 1787, the Constitution was presented to the people of the states. This document has three parts: a preamble; 7 articles outlining the powers and responsibilities of the 3 branches of government; and a section of amendments, the first ten of which are known as the Bill of Rights. The Constitution contains no bills of attainder, meaning that individuals cannot be denied life, liberty, and property without a trial. It does contain the concept of habeas corpus, meaning that arrested individuals must be charged with a crime within 72 hours. Federal judges are to be chosen for life, and there is an electoral college to select the president. In order to be in the House of Representatives, individuals had to be land-owning white males. The Constitution is famous for its system of checks and balances whereby the president can veto Congress, but Congress can override the veto with a 2/3 vote, and the courts can call the acts of either body "unconstitutional."

Ratification process, Federalists and Anti-Federalists
In order for the Constitution to take effect, it had to be ratified by ¾ of the states. The Federalists were those in favor of the Constitution. They were primarily wealthy men who lived along the coast and wanted the commercial protection afforded by a strong federal government. Anti-Federalists, on the other hand, were mainly small farmers and artisans who felt that the Constitution was not truly democratic and would erode the power both of the states and of individuals. The Anti-Federalists wanted a Constitution that allowed for annual elections, a standing army, and a Federal fortress. They also disapproved of the atheism of the document. Unfortunately for the Anti-Federalists, the superior organization of the Federalists helped the Constitution become ratified, despite the fact that most Americans were opposed to it.

Philadelphia Convention of 1787

Although 55 delegates attended the Philadelphia Convention of 1787, only 39 signed the Constitution that emerged from this gathering. The attendees at the convention were exclusively rich men, but were all well-qualified to construct a new government. George Washington presided over the convention, and James Madison (the "father of the Constitution") served as secretary. The representation afforded to the people, as well as to states of different sizes, was a contentious issue throughout. Finally, in what is known as the Great Compromise, it was decided that the lower house (House of Representatives) would be chosen by the people, and the upper house (Senate) would be chosen by the state legislature. This convention also produced the 3/5 compromise, whereby each slave was to be counted as 3/5 of a person. A 20-year moratorium was placed on the slave trade as well. Finally, it was decided at the convention that Congress should have control of commerce and tariffs.

New Republic through Reconstruction

George Washington

Foreign diplomacy under Washington
The United States stayed neutral during the wars of the French Revolution, even issuing a proclamation to that effect in 1793. Meanwhile, the British were constantly testing this neutrality: they did not leave their posts in the Northwest; they seized American ships and forced American sailors into service; and they frequently aided the Native Americans in their conflicts with the United States. This conflict eventually led to the Jay Treaty in 1794 which made the Spanish fear an Anglo-American alliance, causing them to become more willing to discuss American use of the Mississippi River. Pinckney's Treaty, also known as the Treaty of San Lorenzo (1795), gave the United States free use of both the Mississippi and the city of New Orleans.

Washington's Farewell Address and accomplishments
In 1796, Washington decided he was too tired to continue as president. In his famous Farewell Address, he implored the United States to avoid three things: permanent alliances; political factions; and sectionalism. Washington felt that the nation could only be successful if people placed the nation ahead of their own region. For his own part, Washington made some significant improvements during his presidency. He avoided war at a time when the nation was vulnerable. He also avoided political alliances and promoted the national government without alienating great numbers of people. Washington oversaw Hamilton's creation of the economic system and guided expansion to the West (as well as the creation of three new states: Vermont, Kentucky, and Tennessee).

Alexander Hamilton

Hamilton's funding and economic plan for the financial system
The United States was born with $80 million in debt. Alexander Hamilton, however, was not terribly concerned by this; on the contrary, he encouraged credit as a means of financing the rapid capital improvements that would aid economic expansion. Hamilton introduced a funding process, whereby the government would buy back government bonds at full price in order to place money into the economy. Unfortunately, word of this plan leaked to some speculators, who bought the bonds at reduced rates and made huge profits. This led to accusations of a conspiracy. Another aspect of Hamilton's economic plan was for the federal government to assume state debts. This was done in part to tie state governments to the national government.

Custom duties, excise taxes and federal banks
In order to pay off the national debt, Hamilton promoted the Revenue Act of 1789, which was ostensibly a tax on imports, though it amounted to very little. Hamilton hoped to appease American industry with this measure without alienating foreign interests. The Whiskey Tax, instituted in 1791, was another attempt to generate revenue. This tax was wildly unpopular, however, and Washington was forced to call in several state militias to deal with various uprisings. At this time, Hamilton was also trying to establish a national bank, based upon the Bank of England. The Bank of America was established with $10

million in capital and aimed to repay foreign debts, provide a uniform national currency, aid in the collection of taxes, make loans, and act as a federal depository.

Beginning of the Federalist period

After the ratification of the Constitution, George Washington was inaugurated as the first president in New York City. He immediately went outside the Constitution to form the first Cabinet: Thomas Jefferson, Secretary of State; Alexander Hamilton, Secretary of the Treasury; Henry Knox, Secretary of War; Edmund Randolph, Attorney General; and Samuel Osgood, Postmaster General. With the Judiciary Act of 1789, it was decided that there would be 6 justices and one chief justice on the Supreme Court. This act also established the federal court system and the policy of judicial review, whereby federal courts made sure that state courts and laws did not violate the Constitution. This policy was inspired by the case Chisholm v. Georgia, in which the Supreme Court ruled that a citizen of South Carolina could sue the state of Georgia, and that the case must be heard in a Georgia state court.

Rise of the first political parties

Unlike a faction, which exists in order to achieve a single goal, a political party endures beyond the accomplishment of a specific goal. The first two political parties in the United States were the Federalists and the Democratic-Republicans. Hamilton is the primary figure associated with the Federalists, who were wealthy northeasterners in support of a strong central government and a loose interpretation of the Constitution. The Federalists advocated a strong president, the economic policies implemented by Hamilton, and a strong relationship with the British. The Democratic-Republicans, on the other hand, were associated with the so-called "common man" of the South and West. Led by Jefferson and Madison, they advocated a strong central government, a strict interpretation of the Constitution, a close relationship with France, and closely-restricted government spending.

Jay Treaty

The Jay Treaty of 1794 aimed to calm the post-revolution conflicts between Britain and the United States. In it, the British promised to leave their forts in the northwest and to pay for all the recent damages to ships. The British also allowed the US to form a limited commercial treaty with the British West Indies. The Jay Treaty asserted that the rivers and lakes of North America could be used by both Britain and the United States. However, the treaty made no provisions for any future seizures of American ships, and made no mention of Native American attacks on the American frontier. The Southern states were annoyed that the treaty won no compensation for slaves freed during the Revolutionary War, and, moreover, stipulated that Southerners had to repay their pre-war debts. The controversy surrounding the Jay Treaty led to the formation of the first political parties.

Domestic events under Adams

The Alien and Sedition Acts were established in 1798, in part because of xenophobia arising from conflict with the French. The Alien Act increased the number of years before one could obtain citizenship, gave the president the power to deport anyone and allowed the president to jail dangerous aliens during times of war. The Sedition Act made it a crime to libel or slander US officials or policies; many people believed this policy was a violation of First Amendment rights. The Virginia and Kentucky Resolves, promoted by Jefferson and

Madison, stated that a contact exists between the state and national governments, but that the national government had exceeded its authority and broken the contract. This document advocated that states should have the power of nullification over national policies; only Virginia and Kentucky supported this policy, which had the potential to fatally undermine the Constitution.

Federalist period

The Federalist period had some remarkable successes and some bitter failures. It saw the establishment of the national bank and the Treasury system under Hamilton. The United States, amazingly, was able to pay off all of its debt during this period. The Federalist administration can also be credited with maintaining international neutrality, establishing the Pinckney Treaty, crushing the Whiskey Rebellion, and getting the British out of their northwest posts. On the other hand, over time the Federalists became known as an elitist party, and the Alien and Sedition Acts were very unpopular. The Jay Treaty was seen as a diplomatic failure by most Americans, and in general the Federalists were not able to maintain very cordial relations with Europe (especially France).

John Adams

Election of Adams and the conflict with the French during Adams presidency
John Adams became the second president of the United States in the election of 1796; his opponent, Thomas Jefferson, became vice president because he received the second-most electoral votes. Adams was immediately confronted by the French, who were angry about the Jay Treaty and the broken Treaty of Alliance of 1788. After the French began destroying American ships, Adams sent American diplomats to meet with the French ambassador Talleyrand, who demanded tribute and then snubbed the Americans. There followed an undeclared naval war between 1798 and 1800. During which, the American military grew rapidly, warships were built and the Department of the Navy was established. Finally, at the Convention of 1800, the Treaty of Alliance of 1778 was torn up and it was agreed in this new Treaty of Mortefontaine that the Americans would pay for damages done to their ships by the French, among a host of other clauses including each country giving the other Most Favored Nation trade status.

Election of 1800

In the election of 1800, the Federalists were represented by John Adams and C.C. Pinckney, and the Democratic-Republicans by Thomas Jefferson and Aaron Burr. The Federalists had been weakened both by the unpopularity of the Alien and Sedition Acts and the internal feud between Adams and Hamilton. They therefore focused their campaign on Jefferson, accusing him of being an atheist, of stealing money from the poor and of having an affair with a slave. In the election, Jefferson finished with the same number of electoral votes as his supposed running mate, Burr, who surprisingly refused to concede. This situation led to the 12th amendment, which states that a candidate must stipulate his desired office. Jefferson finally won the tie-breaking vote in the House of Representatives, sweeping the Federalists out of office.

Marbury v. Madison

William Marbury was one of the Federalist judges removed from office by the Judiciary Act of 1802. Marbury, having been promised a job, brought up the issue with James Madison, who pleaded ignorance. The issue became contentious and in 1803 came before the Supreme Court as Marbury v. Madison. Although Section XIII of the Judiciary Act of 1789 had a Writ of Mandamus which required Madison to honor the appointment, Chief Justice John Marshall declared this section unconstitutional. This was a historic act: although the power of the Supreme Court to declare state and local measures unconstitutional had been established, this had never before been done on the national level. Marshall thereby established an independent judiciary; he is quoted as saying, "The Constitution is the supreme Law of the Land, with the Supreme Court as the final interpreter."

Jeffersonian Republicans

After using his inauguration speech to try to pacify angry Federalists, Thomas Jefferson went on to introduce the "spoils system," replacing Federalist office-holders with Republicans. He also reversed many of the Federalist policies: the Alien Act was repealed, and the Sedition Act expired in 1801 (everyone arrested under its authority was pardoned, absolved, and had their fines repaid). Jefferson also sought to reform the judiciary. The Judiciary Act of 1801, otherwise known as the Circuit Court Act, was passed by the Federalists in order to cement some of their judges in place; Jefferson in turn forced through the Judiciary Act of 1802, which removed all 42 of these judges.

Foreign policy under the Jeffersonian Republicans
The most important event during the dominance of the Jeffersonian Republicans was the War of 1812, fought between France and Britain. In the United States, there was much speculation as to whether the young nation would side with the shark (Britain) or the tiger (France). In 1803, Jefferson had declared American ships neutral, an act which annoyed both sides. The British subsequently passed the Orders-in-Council, and the French the Berlin and Milan Decrees, all of which were designed to weaken American shipping in Europe. The US responded with the Non-Importation Act of 1806, though this was largely a failure. In 1807, an American ship called the Chesapeake was attacked by a British ship, leading Jefferson to issue the Embargo Act of 1807. This act forbade American ships from leaving for foreign ports; it was very unpopular, and was repealed in 1809.

Treaty of Ildefonso and the Louisiana Purchase

In an agreement between the French and Spanish known alternately as the *Treaty of Ildefonso* or the *Retrocession*, Napoleon Bonaparte acquired Louisiana. This, along with Spain's closing of New Orleans to American business, made Jefferson nervous, and he thus sent James Monroe to France in order to purchase New Orleans and West Florida. Bonaparte, himself made anxious by a rebellion in Haiti and a renewal of hostilities with the British, signed over 800,000 square miles to the US, making the *Louisiana Purchase* the largest land acquisition without bloodshed in human history. Napoleon hoped to curry favor with the United States, in order to forestall a possible Anglo-American alliance.

Perception of the Louisiana Purchase
The Louisiana Purchase was probably the high point of Jefferson's presidency; it was seen at home as a diplomatic victory that also avoided drawing the United States into conflict with

the European powers. It destroyed the Federalist party. After the Louisiana Purchase was completed, explorers set out to discover just what had been bought; among these explorers were Meriwether Lewis and William Clark. Meanwhile, the United States began to make inroads into Spanish-controlled West Florida. In 1810, rebels attacked Baton Rouge and James Madison claimed that West Florida was now part of the US. Of course, the Spanish protested, but they were unable to reestablish themselves. In 1818, Andrew Jackson would lead a group of soldiers into East Florida under the pretense of taming the Seminoles. In 1819, the Spanish would reluctantly sign the Treaty of Onis, in which the US formally acquired East Florida for $5 million, which the Spanish promptly returned to pay off some of their debt to the US.

Yazoo Claims and John Randolph

In 1795, the corrupt Georgia legislature sold some land known as the Yazoo Claims for almost nothing to a group of northeastern speculators in exchange for a bribe. When a new group of legislators came into office in 1797, they revoked the land sales, infuriating the speculators. In 1802, the land claims were ceded to the national government and Jefferson decided to grant the speculators a cash settlement. John Randolph, however, was the chairman of the House committee responsible for paying this settlement, and he refused to make the payment, stating that the deal was "bathed in corruption." Though the Supreme Court eventually granted the settlements in the case Fletcher v. Peck (1810), Randolph was permanently alienated from Jefferson and went on to form a group called the Tertium Quids. This group was the ultra-conservative pro-states' rights contingent of the Democratic-Republicans.

Aaron Burr

After losing his challenge for the presidency in 1800, Aaron Burr was left out of the 1804 election and became embittered. He then lost a bid for the governorship of New York, in part because of the mudslinging of Alexander Hamilton. At this point, Burr began to toy with the idea of forming a new country in the West. Hamilton, hearing of this plan, informed Jefferson. Burr promptly challenged Hamilton to a duel, and in 1806 killed him at Weehawken, NJ. Burr headed west, and planned to start a new country in Louisiana and the areas controlled by Spain. Jefferson formally charged Burr with treason, but, citing executive privilege, refused to attend the trial. Burr was eventually found not guilty, in part because he had only planned a new country, and in part because the US was unable to find any reliable witnesses.

Madison and "peaceful coercion"

In the 1808 election, James Madison of the Democrat-Republicans easily defeated C.C. Pinckney. Madison continued Jefferson's policy of "peaceful coercion" with respect to France and Britain, but the lack of an organized American military made it difficult for him to get the attention of these major powers. In 1809, Madison convinced Congress to pass the Non-Intercourse Act of 1809, which forbade trade with Britain and France until they began treating American business fairly. When the British ambassador David Erskine vowed to improve the treatment of American businesses, Madison agreed to trade with England. However, Erskine's superior quickly overruled him, making Madison look ridiculous and souring Anglo-American relations further.

War of 1812

Controversy surrounding the War of 1812

The conservative members of Madison's party, known as the Tertium Quids, opposed the War of 1812 because they felt it would be too expensive, would result in the perpetuation of a standing army, would damage America economically, and would lead to the acquisition of Canada as a slave state. These critics were opposed in Congress by the Warhawks, so-called by the Federalists to imply that they were picking a fight. The Warhawks mainly represented the Southwest and the West, and included luminaries such as Henry Clay, John C. Calhoun, and Felix Grundy. They supported the war because they thought it would bolster foreign trade, would discourage the British from inciting Native Americans along the frontier, and could result in land gain. In selling the war to the American people, Madison stressed the British insult to American honor; he mentioned several stories about impressments of Americans into British military service.

Events leading up to combat in War of 1812

Despite a great deal of bloated rhetoric both for and against the war, the US fought against Britain for a few basic reasons, namely to gain more land and to destroy alliances between the British and Native Americans. Americans had become incensed when, following his defeat to the Americans at Tippecanoe Creek, Chief Tecumseh had fled north into British-controlled Canada. This provocation provided enough popular support to declare war. Unfortunately, the American military was both unprepared and overconfident. Most American military strategists thought it would be quite easy to take Canada, but the army had only 35,000 troops at the time. Moreover, the first Bank of the United States had just gone defunct, and so there were scarce economic resources to support a war.

Major battles of War of 1812

At the Battle of Lake Erie in September of 1813, the American Commander Perry secured Detroit for the US. At the Battle of Lake Champlain, the American General Thomas McDonough secured northern New York from British invasion. At the Battle of the Thames, the American General William Henry Harrison defeated a coalition of British and Native American forces; Tecumseh was killed. Andrew Jackson scored a decisive victory at the Battle of Horseshoe Bend. During this war, much of Washington, DC (including the White House) was torched. A crucial point of the war came when the US was able to successfully defend Fort McHenry, outside of Baltimore; this conflict inspired Francis Scott Key's composition of "The Star-spangled Banner." At the Battle of New Orleans, Andrew Jackson used a rag-tag collection of soldiers and pirates to defeat the British navy.

Significance of the War of 1812

The War of 1812 did not really accomplish its supposed goal of establishing neutral trading rights for American ships. The exodus of Napoleon during the war made this a moot point. Nevertheless, from Madison's perspective the war could only be seen as a major success. The United States lost no major territory, and scored enough victories to keep the British from making any extreme demands. More importantly, perhaps, Americans were overjoyed that the US was finally getting respect from the major European powers. Nationalism exploded in the US: people forgot the debacle of the failed national bank, and the economy boomed. Finally, the success of the War of 1812 effectively drove the final nail into the coffin of the Federalist party.

Conclusion of the War of 1812

Throughout the War of 1812, there was loud opposition from the Federalists in the northeast. At the Hartford Convention, they formally blamed Madison for the war, and proposed changes to the Constitution whereby a 2/3 vote would be needed for declaring war and for admitting new states to the union. The War of 1812 required several agreements to fully restore relations between the US and Britain. The Treaty of Ghent returned Anglo-American ties to their pre-war terms, and proposed that commissions be created to settle differences. The Rush-Bagot Treaty of 1817 formally declared that there would be no naval race between the 2 countries. At the Convention of 1818, a line was drawn along the 49th parallel, dividing Canada from Louisiana, and it was declared that the 2 countries would jointly occupy Oregon. In the Adams-Onis Treaty of 1819, a western boundary for Louisiana was set, and the Spanish renounced their claims to Oregon.

Non-Intercourse Act of 1809 replaced

Madison replaced the Non-Intercourse Act of 1809 with Macon's Bill No. 2, which declared that America would be open to trade with any country. The bill also stipulated that if either Britain or France agreed to neutral trading rights with the US, the US would immediately cease trade with the other. France jumped at this opportunity, and the US cut diplomatic ties with Britain. The British, weakened by the American embargoes and by a bitter winter, rescinded the Orders-in-council, although the US had already declared war upon them. After the British Prime Minister was assassinated, the new foreign secretary, Castlereigh, tried to mend relations, but the US went to war anyway. The War of 1812 was very unpopular, especially among Federalists in the northeast. Many Americans felt that England could not be beaten, that engaging in a war would damage US business, and that Napoleon was not a very savory ally.

Triumph of Neo-Federalism

In 1816, Madison declared that that the government should increase the army, the national debt, and the banking interests, an agenda oddly reminiscent of Federalism. The Second Bank of the United States was shown to be necessary by the War of 1812, but it was poorly organized and came to be known as a "moneyed monster." The Tariff of 1816 was established to protect fledgling industry; it was as popular in the northeast as it was unpopular in the south. Much of the tariff money went to developing infrastructure; the new method of paving invented by John MacAdam enabled the creation of long thoroughfares, mostly in the north. It was even proposed in the so-called "Bonus Bill" that all of the surplus money from the new bank should go to the roads; Madison vetoed this measure to avoid further alienating the south.

Strengthening of American national identity

The success of the War of 1812 and the prospering economy made Madison extremely popular. In the northeast, with the implementation of the British factory system, and in the southeast, with the invention of the cotton gin, manufacturing interests were booming. This sense of national identity was strengthened by the emergence of the United States' first generation of post-colonial artists. In literature, James Fenimore Cooper and Washington Irving (*The Legend of Sleepy Hollow*) were eminent. A uniquely American style of architecture developed, led by Jefferson, among others, emphasizing columns, symmetry, and classical proportions. The Hudson River school produced a group of painters influenced by the natural beauty of their region; among them John James Audubon.

Missouri Compromise

In 1820, the territory called Missouri asked to enter the union as a slave state. This would have made the number of slave states 12, to 11 free states. Rather than allow this to happen, William Talmadge abolished slavery in Missouri. Henry Clay then offered another solution, known as the Missouri Compromise. According to this proposal, Missouri would enter the union as a slave state, but Maine would separate from Massachusetts and become a free state. Furthermore, everything south of Missouri would be slave territory, and everything above would be free. This compromise was satisfactory, even though the proposed free lands were larger than the slave lands. This was because most agreed that slavery could not be successful in colder climates and because many thought that Texas would soon be a part of the United States.

The Era of Good Feelings

In the election of 1816, the Democrat-Republican James Monroe defeated the last Federalist candidate, Rufus King, by a landslide. The Federalist opposition to the War of 1812 doomed the party to extinction. Monroe's early term was not without its problems, however. A mild depression caused by over-speculation on western lands led to the Panic of 1819, and began a 20-year boom-bust cycle. These problems were exacerbated by the Second Bank of the United States; the Bank's pressure on the so-called "wildcat" banks to foreclose on properties, as well as the unwillingness of the Bank to loan money, made it very unpopular. The nationalism generated by the War of 1812 was damaged by these economic travails.

Monroe Doctrine

After a series of revolutions in Latin America, the United States was the first to recognize the sovereignty of the new countries. This was in part because the revolutionaries had used the United States as inspiration, in part because the US preferred to have weak, independent nations nearby, and in part because the US wanted to maintain and expand its lucrative trade with Latin America. The British attempted to persuade the US to sign an agreement preventing foreign intervention in Latin America, but Monroe decided to maintain American independence and issue his own document. This document, known as the Monroe Doctrine, had as its two main principles non-intervention and non-colonization. Many considered it a "paper tiger," because it was really only as effective as the American ability to enforce it. Still, it seemed to encourage foreign nations to come to the bargaining table rather than test the American military.

Marshall court

The Supreme Court led by John Marshall is credited with increasing the power of the national government over that of the states. This court also gave the judicial branch more power and prestige, notably in the case of Marbury v. Madison (1803). Marshall was known as an arch-Federalist, and as a loose interpreter of the Constitution. In the case McCullough v. Maryland (1819), the court ruled that a national bank is allowed by the Constitution, and that states cannot tax a federal agency. In the case of Gibbons v. Ogden (1824), the right of Congress to regulate interstate commerce was reaffirmed, and indeed federal regulation of

- 24 -

just about anything was made possible. In Fletcher v. Peck (1810), the sanctity of contracts was asserted; this case also established the right of the Supreme Court to declare state laws unconstitutional.

John Quincy Adams

Election of 1824 and Adams' administration
All the major candidates in the 1824 election were Democrat-Republicans. Although Andrew Jackson received more electoral votes than John Quincy Adams, he did not win a majority, and Adams (with the help of Henry Clay) won the run-off in the House of Representatives. Adams was a fierce nationalist at a time when many in the country were sectionalist. Although his initiatives for a national university and public funding for the arts were well-meaning, Adams was still believed to be out of touch with the common man. He further alienated the middle and lower classes with the Tariff of 1828, known in the South as the "Tariff of Abominations." The South was already on shaky economic ground and the tariff became a scapegoat for its troubles. John C. Calhoun was an especially ardent Southern voice; he futilely proposed that states should have the ability to nullify federal regulations.

Andrew Jackson

Jacksonian democracy in the 1820s and 30s
The 1820s and 30s are known as the era of Jacksonian democracy, which was political rather than economic or social. Jackson was considered to be emblematic of the "common man." In the years after the conclusion of the War of 1812, it was generally considered that America was "safe for democracy," and thus suffrage was extended to poor people in many states. As more people became involved in politics, campaigning became more about image and perception than the issues. This change also ended the tradition known as "King Caucus," in which candidates were chosen by a small group of powerful men; now, candidates were to be selected by a series of primaries and nominating conventions. Furthermore, the members of the electoral college would be chosen by the voters rather than by the state legislature. The new system maintained the tradition of patronage (the spoils system), in which newly-elected officials would fill the government offices with their supporters.

Andrew Jackson is often seen as a symbol of the rising power of the New West, or as an embodiment of the "rags to riches" fable. He spent much of his presidency trying to promote the idea of nationalism at a time when most of the country was ardently sectionalist. During his presidency, he dominated Congress, vetoing more legislation than all of the previous presidents combined. He was also famous for his so-called "Kitchen Cabinet," a group of close advisers without official positions. Many of these men later received formal appointments, including as Secretary of State (Martin van Buren), Postmaster General (Amos Kendall), and Secretary of the Treasury (Roger B. Taney).

Election of 1828
The election of 1828 is considered the first modern campaign in American politics. Andrew Jackson had the first campaign manager, Amos Kendall, and produced buttons, posters, and slogans to support his candidacy. These men—Jackson, Kendall, John C. Calhoun, and Martin van Buren—formed the beginning of the Democratic party. Meanwhile, the incumbent John Quincy Adams ran a very formal campaign, with little of the "flesh-pressing"

of Jackson. Adams tried to discredit Jackson as an adulterer and bigamist because Jackson's wife had not been officially divorced at the time of their marriage. When his wife died during the campaign, however, the popular sentiment returned to Jackson, and he won the election by a considerable margin. Jackson's inauguration was an over-crowded, chaotic affair; the president suffered three cracked ribs during the festivities.

Tariff of 1832 and Force Act of 183

At a feast in celebration of Thomas Jefferson—a man noted for his nationalism—Andrew Jackson promoted the idea of the nation, saying, "Our Union, it must be preserved." John C. Calhoun responded with a speech in which he referred to "Our Union, next to our liberty most dear," indicating that the South was not going to back down. The milder Tariff of 1832 was then offered by Jackson to appease the South and Calhoun; instead, Southern politicians declared it was not enough, and Calhoun resigned from Congress in order to organize the opposition to all tariffs. Henry Clay, who realized that Jackson could easily overpower South Carolina, was further disturbed by the Force Act of 1832, which stated that the president had the right to use military force to keep a state in the union. So, Clay proposed an even lower Compromise Tariff of 1833: the tariff would be lowered from 35% to 20-25% over the next ten years. Both sides agreed to this compromise.

Raid into Florida and Webster-Hayne debate

One of the least successful events in Jackson's presidency was a raid into Florida in 1828, made for the purpose of subduing the Seminoles. The raid did not go well, and even Jackson's Secretary of War, John C. Calhoun, referred to it as "idiotic." Another major event in Jackson's term was the Webster-Hayne debate of 1829-30, held to debate western expansion. The senators of the northeast were opposed to western migration, mainly because they felt it would weaken manufacturing and create a new political rival. Senator Robert Hayne of South Carolina blasted the war record of the Northeast, in the hopes of allying the West and the South. Daniel Webster (MA) retorted that the US is not a collection of states, but a union that happens to be divided into states; he asserted that if states could nullify federal measures, the only thing holding the union together was a "rope of sand."

Bank War of 1836

It had already been arranged that the renewal of the Second Bank of America would be discussed in 1836. It was common knowledge that Jackson hated the Bank, and thus Henry Clay and others tried to renew it ahead of time, in 1832. Jackson was then forced to assert his position: he declared that the bank was anti-West, anti-American, unconstitutional and a "monopoly of money." The unpopularity of Clay's attempt to renew the Bank was a main reason that he was crushed by Jackson in the 1832 election. After making sure that the Bank would not be renewed, Jackson sought to mend fences with the Northeast by avidly promoting the Union. This was Jackson's genius as a politician; he always was careful to get what he wanted without fully alienating any faction.

Maysville Road veto and Native American removal

In 1830, Jackson set a precedent by vetoing the funding of a road that was to be entirely within one state (Kentucky). Many believed that Jackson vetoed this bill to spite Henry Clay, but the move had some positive political consequences as well: the Southerners appreciated the idea that states should tend to their own business and northerners liked it because the road would have given people easier access to the West. Jackson's attempts at relocating Native Americans were less successful. The passage of the Indian Resettlement Act of 1830 was the first attempt by the national government to force migration. In the case of

Worcester v. Georgia (1832), the Supreme Court ruled against those who sought to grab Native lands. John Marshall asserted that the Cherokee nation was sovereign, but a ward of the US. Despite Marshall's assertion of Native American rights, Jackson supported the slow and steady conquest of land in the South and West.

John Tyler

John Tyler, a Virginia aristocrat, was the first vice president to take over in mid-term. Oddly, even though he was the Whig candidate, he opposed almost all of the Whig agenda. Henry Clay hoped to dominate Tyler, but his attempts to create a third national bank and to improve infrastructure in the West were both vetoed by Tyler. Tyler's presidency was also fraught with conflict with the British; he endured the Lumberjacks' War of 1842 and the Hunters' Lodges skirmishes in 1838, both of which were minor conflicts along the Canadian border. There was also the incident of the Caroline, an American ship sunk by the British for allegedly smuggling supplies to Canadian rebels. In the Webster-Ashburton Treaty of 1842 fugitives were exchanged, the border of Maine was set at the St. John River and it was established that the British could no longer search American ships.

Martin Van Buren

Election of 1836 and the Van Buren presidency
When Jackson decided not to pursue a third term as president, his vice president Martin Van Buren ran and won over a group of challengers including the Whig candidate William Henry Harrison. Van Buren's presidency was marked by frequent border disputes with Canada. Also, Van Buren suffered through the Panic of 1837; like in 1819, this was caused by over-speculation in the West. In the 1836 "Specie Circular," Jackson had declared that all land bought from the government must be paid for in gold coins. Because gold was hard to come by, many people lost their property. Further economic problems were created by over-spending on infrastructure in many states. One of the results of Van Buren's handling of the situation was that it became acceptable for the president to influence the amount of money in circulation. In 1840, a listless Van Buren was defeated by Harrison, who promptly died after a month as president. John Tyler became the next president.

Texas' role in US expansion

In 1821, Mexico received its independence from Spain. Mexico sold Texan lands to Americans, yet these people were still required to live under Mexican civil law (for one thing, people had to convert to Catholicism). In 1832, however, Santa Anna led a coup in Mexico and decided to crack down on the Texans. This led to the Texas Revolution of 1836, in which Texan General William Travis' men were massacred by the forces of Santa Anna at the Alamo, in which both Davy Crockett and Jim Bowie were killed. After suffering some other defeats the Texans, led by Sam Houston, finally defeated Santa Anna at the Battle of San Jacinto in 1836 and he was forced below the Rio Grande. Nevertheless, Texas was not made part of the US, mainly because the issue of slavery was so contentious at the time.

Manifest Destiny

The phrase "manifest destiny," meaning the inevitability and righteousness of the American expansion westward, was coined by the editor John O'Sullivan. This idea was lent further credence by the work of Horace Greeley, the journalist responsible for the admonition, "Go

West, young man!" Besides this mythology, however, there were some sound reasons why the United States expanded westward. For one thing, there was cheap and fertile land in the west, and the more that was claimed by the Americans, the less which could be claimed by the British. Americans also had an eye towards claiming the western ports to begin trading with Asia. Finally, many Americans felt that they would only be benefiting the world by spreading their ideals of liberty and democracy across as much land as possible.

James K. Polk

The election of 1844 brought to the forefront a number of critical issues; the economy was still hurting from the Panic of 1837, there was growing support for abolitionism and the issue of manifest destiny was gaining steam. Somewhat surprisingly, the bland North Carolinian James K. Polk defeated Henry Clay and succeeded John Tyler as president. He instituted the Walker Tariff, which lowered the rate at which foreign goods were taxed from 35% to 25%. He also reinstated the Independent Sub-Treasury system in 1846. Mainly, however, Polk's presidency is associated with westward expansion; Texas was brought into the union as a slave state in December of 1845. Polk also spent considerable time trying to get possession of Oregon.

Salt Lake City, Oregon, and California

The territory of Oregon became more important to the US government as fur-trapping became a lucrative industry. Oregon was also known to contain rich farmland. As for California, its natural bounty had been described by whalers since the 1820s. In the 1840s, whole families (including the ill-fated Donner party) began to migrate there. Around this time the Church of Jesus Christ of Latter-day Saints, otherwise known as the Mormon Church, was founded by Joseph Smith. Among the beliefs espoused by the Mormons were polygamy, communalism and the abolition of slavery. After Smith's death, the Mormons were led by Brigham Young and settled in what is now Salt Lake City. Meanwhile, in 1848 gold was discovered in a California stream, generating still more excitement over the economic potential of the West.

Mexican War

The United States scored major victories over Mexico at Buena Vista, where they were led by Zachary Taylor, and Vera Cruz, where they were led by Winfield Scott. The American effort in New Mexico was led by Stephen Kearney and in California by John C. Fremont. The Treaty of Guadalupe-Hidalgo was signed in 1848 after Polk sent an emissary with cash in an effort to persuade Santa Anna to stop the war. Under the terms of the treaty, the US got California, the rest of Texas, and all of the Mexican territory between Louisiana and California (including what would become Utah and Nevada). In exchange, the US erased a good deal of Mexico's debts. Controversy immediately erupted over whether the new territories would be allowed to have slaves; some abolitionists wanted to cancel the treaty while some Southern Democrats wanted to claim the entirety of Mexico.

Causes of the Mexican War
The immediate causes of the Mexican War were the American annexation of Texas, disputes over the Southern border of Texas and the large amount of money owed to the United States by Mexico. Moreover, it was well known that the Mexicans held the US in contempt, considering them greedy land-grabbers. Polk sent an emissary to buy Texas, California, and

some Mexican territory for $30 million; he was refused. Zachary Taylor then led an American expedition into a disputed area of Texas where some of them were killed. Polk was able to use these deaths as a rationale for war, despite considerable opposition in Congress. Overall, the Democrats supported the war, while the Whigs, led in part by Abraham Lincoln, were opposed.

Gold rush and the Compromise of 1850

After Zachary Taylor won the election of 1848, he immediately had to deal with the issue of slavery in the new western territories. This issue was magnified by the California gold rush. Taylor declared that all of the lands would be free, enraging the Southerners. Soon after, however, Taylor died of food poisoning and was succeeded by Vice-president Millard Fillmore. In order to solve the problem of slavery in the west, Henry Clay proposed the so-called Compromise of 1850: California would be a free state, while New Mexico would be allowed to decide for itself; there would be no more slave trading in the District of Columbia; there would be tighter laws regarding fugitive slaves; and Texas would receive $10 million for its lost territories. Fillmore readily signed this agreement, but problems with it arose immediately. One of which was that the Underground Railroad of Harriet Tubman was already making it very difficult to catch fugitive slaves.

Road to Civil War

There was immense controversy surrounding the slavery policy in the new American territories after the war with Mexico: Polk wanted to simply extend the line of the Missouri Compromise out to the Pacific while abolitionists offered the Wilmot Proviso, which declared that none of the territories should have slaves. The Southern states felt slavery should be allowed, and a more moderate view was offered by Stephen Douglas, who declared that the people of the new states should decide whether they wanted slavery or not. In the election of 1848, the war-hero Zachary Taylor (Whig) defeated Lewis Cass (Democrat) and the former president Martin Van Buren (Free Soil party, a collection of abolitionist interests).

Trans-Continental Railroad, Ostend Manifesto, and Kansas-Nebraska Act

The construction of the Trans-Continental Railroad was begun in 1853 for the purpose of transporting easterners to California. With the Gadsden Purchase, the US had purchased some New Mexican lands so that the train could avoid the mountains. With the Ostend Manifesto in 1854, the US attempted to purchase Cuba from Spain for $120 million; Spain refused, and though the US threatened to take the island by force, they never did (in part because it was believed that the South wanted to make it a slave state). The Kansas-Nebraska Act (1854), authored by Stephen Douglas, divided the Nebraska territory into two parts (Kansas and Nebraska) and declared that slavery would be determined by popular sovereignty in those territories. This act drove northerners to the liberal side and caused the creation of the Republican party. The opposing factions engaged in violence to try and win the popular vote. Though Kansas worded its constitution in an attempt to have slaves, the document fell apart upon review by Congress, and Kansas entered as a free state.

Election of 1852 and the growing crisis of slavery

In the election of 1852, Democrat Franklin Pierce easily defeated the Whig Winfield Scott who was hurt by his association with the abolitionist William H. Seward. At this time, despite the growing crisis of slavery, there were some positive changes in the US. One was that the introduction of California as a free state permanently upset the sectional balance. Immigration into the Northeastern cities was bringing a wealth of new ideas. The northern states resisted the fugitive slave laws by passing initiatives in support of personal liberties and by aiding the Underground Railroad. Harriet Beecher Stowe enraged the South with her novel Uncle Tom's Cabin (1852). In 1857, Hinton R. Helper published "The Impending Crisis of the South," an essay that suggested the South was becoming a slave to the North because of its reactionary view on slavery.

Lincoln-Douglas debates

During the campaign to become senator of Illinois in 1858, Abraham Lincoln and Stephen Douglas eloquently debated the issue of slavery. In the so-called Freeport Doctrine, Lincoln questioned whether the people of a territory could vote against slavery. The Supreme Court would say no, but Lincoln wondered whether the people should not have the final say. Douglas essentially agreed, stating that the people of the territory should decide. Douglas won the election, though his stance on slavery irritated Southerners. In 1859, the abolitionist John Brown led a raid on a federal arsenal at Harper's Ferry, Virginia. Brown's group was only able to take a fire station, and Brown himself was captured and executed by a battalion led by Robert E. Lee. Brown became a martyr to the North.

Sumner-Brooks Incident

In 1856, Senator Charles Sumner (MA) gave an impassioned speech on the "Crime against Kansas," in which he blamed the south for the violence. One of the men whom he singled out for blame was the uncle of Senator Preston Brooks (SC); Brooks beat Sumner with his walking stick, and was glorified in the South. In the election of 1856, James Buchanan (Democrat) defeated several candidates, including Millard Fillmore (American party; some southern states had threatened to secede should Fillmore prevail). Next came the Dred Scott case. Scott was a slave taken to a free state by his owner, and then transported back to a slave state. Abolitionists said he should be a free man. The Supreme Court, however, ruled that slaves are property and can be transported across state lines without being changed. This decision effectively rendered the Kansas-Nebraska Act, the Missouri Compromise, and the whole idea of popular sovereignty unconstitutional.

Compromises to save the Union

The US government made a number of compromises in an attempt to preserve the Union after Lincoln's election. The Crittenden Compromise extended the line of the Missouri Compromise and promised federal protection of slavery south of that line. The House of Representatives Compromise offered an extension of the Missouri Compromise and a Constitutional amendment to protect slavery. The Virginia Peace Convention produced an offer to extend the line of the Missouri Compromise and establish that slavery can never be outlawed except by the permission of the owner. Finally, Congress offered $300 for each slave. The South said that this was not enough money and the North was appalled by the offer, regardless.

Election of 1860 and the secession of the South

In the election of 1860, Abraham Lincoln defeated three other challengers. Lincoln's platform was anti-slavery, though he vowed to leave it intact where it already existed. He also promised full rights to immigrants, the completion of a Pacific Railroad, free homesteads, and a protective tariff. After the election, South Carolina seceded, followed by the rest of the Deep South (Mississippi, Alabama, Georgia, Louisiana, Florida and Texas). These states established the Confederate States of America, with its capital in Montgomery, Alabama. The president of the CSA was Jefferson Davis. Outgoing US President Buchanan claimed that he had no constitutional authority to stop the secession, but upon entering office Lincoln attempted to maintain control of all Southern forts. This led to the firing on Ft. Sumter (SC) by the Confederates. As Lincoln called for aid, the Upper South (Virginia, Arkansas, North Carolina and Tennessee) seceded as well, and the CSA made Richmond, Virginia its new capital.

Advantages of the North in the Civil War

The Northern side in the Civil War contained 22 states with 22 million people. The North also contained most of the US' coal, iron, and copper, as well as 92% of the industry. The Union side had more than twice as much railroad track as the Confederacy and a vastly larger navy. Most importantly, perhaps, the Union had a huge advantage in troops. Most of the Northern troops were either volunteers or had been conscripted (starting in 1863). It was permissible to pay someone to take your space in the military. The North generally had between 2 and 3 times as many troops as the South during the war. The South was really only able to survive for so long because it fought a very defensive war.

Why the Civil War was fought

The Civil War was fought for a number of reasons, but the most important of these was the controversy about slavery. The issue of slavery touched on moral, economic, and political themes. Also, the differing geography of the North and South had caused the latter to develop an economy that they felt could only survive through slavery. The Civil War also sprang from the ongoing debate over states' rights; many in the South felt that states should have the power to nullify federal regulations and believed that the North had too much representation in Congress; and, indeed, the North had received much more federal aid for infrastructure. Finally, there was a general difference in culture between the North and South; the North was more of a dynamic and democratic society, while the South was more of a static oligarchy.

Military strategies of the North and South during the Civil War

The North began the Civil War by trying to blockade the Southern coast and seal off the border states; they hoped to end the war quickly by preventing supplies from reaching the Confederacy. The North also wanted to divide the South into two parts by seizing control of the Mississippi River. This plan would later be adjusted, and Sherman's March would try to divide the South into a northern and southern half. The Confederacy, meanwhile, knew that its best chance for success was to fight defensively (the South did not want any Northern territory). They also knew that they would need help from European powers. The South hoped to outlast the North's will to fight, to capture Washington, DC, and to receive Maryland into the Confederacy.

Advantages and disadvantages of the Confederacy

The Confederate States of America was comprised of 11 states with only 9 million people. When the war began, the South had no organized army or navy. At first, the troops were strictly volunteers, but eventually the CSA established a draft to bolster the ranks. The Confederacy did have some advantages, however. One was that they were fighting on their own soil and thus they already had interior lines of defense as well as knowledge of the terrain. On the whole, the Confederate commanders were more experienced and talented. Finally, the Confederacy had a psychological advantage over the North: they were fighting for a tangible reason (namely, to preserve their lives and property, while the North had to motivate its troops with notions of "preserving the Union."

Antietam and the Emancipation Proclamation

At the Battle of Antietam (MD) in September of 1862, the Confederate General Robert E. Lee went on the offensive, hoping to bring Maryland into the Confederacy, sever the channels between Washington, DC and the North, and attract the recognition of the European powers. This was the bloodiest battle of the Civil War and ended in a draw. It was after this battle that Lincoln issued his famous Emancipation Proclamation. This document freed the slaves in any area that was taken by the Union, or in areas from which slaves could enter the Union. It did not, however, free slaves in the Border States, because Lincoln wanted to maintain loyalty to the Union in these areas. The aims of the Emancipation Proclamation were three: to keep the British from assisting the South, to motivate the Northern troops and to effect a positive moral change.

Major battles of the Civil War

The *First Battle of Bull Run* was fought in Manassas, VA in July of 1861. The North believed that an easy victory here would allow them to quickly take Richmond. Washingtonians even picnicked around the battlefield, anticipating a pleasant spectacle. It was not to be, however: led by Stonewall Jackson (who actually earned that nickname at this battle), the South won a shocking victory. As a result, the South became somewhat overconfident, and the North realized it was in for a long war. At the *Battle of Shiloh* (TN) in April of 1862, Ulysses S. Grant led the Union to its first major victory. At the *Second Battle of Bull Run* in August of 1862, Stonewall Jackson again defeated a Northern army, this time with the help of Robert E. Lee.

The Union General mounted a siege against the crucial Confederate city of *Vicksburg* (MS) in July of 1863. When the Confederates had finally been starved into surrender, the Union had total control of the Mississippi River. Then, between July and October of 1864, the major Southern rail hub of Atlanta was conquered and burned by Union troops under General William Sherman. This victory guaranteed that Lincoln would be reelected in the election of 1864. It also marked the beginning of *Sherman's March to the Sea*, a campaign of devastation mounted by the Union in late 1864 and early 1865. Sherman's troops melted Southern rails and destroyed Southern crops and factories, creating a swath of chaos that stretched from Atlanta to Savannah.

At the *Battle of Fredericksburg* (VA) in December of 1862, Robert E. Lee successfully repelled the attacks of the Union General Burnside. At the *Battle of Chancellorsville* (VA) in May of 1863, Lee scored his greatest victory of the war; it was during this battle, however, that the Confederate General Stonewall Jackson was mortally wounded by his own troops. At the *Battle of Gettysburg* (PA) in July of 1863, the Confederacy troops led by Lee suffered a damaging defeat. Lee had hoped to take some pressure off the South with a successful surge into the North, but instead got caught in an unfavorable tactical position and endured massive casualties. Most historians believe the Union victory at Gettysburg was the turning point in the war.

Lincoln's Reconstruction plan

According to Lincoln, the relation between the North and the South after the completion of the Civil War would include "malice for none, charity for all." He imagined that the President would lead the Reconstruction effort, and, in 1863, he vowed that once 10% of the 1860 voters in a Southern state pledged loyalty to the Union, they could draft a new state constitution and receive "executive recognition." Lincoln was unsure whether blacks should be gradually emancipated or relocated, but he knew they should be free. As for his own Republican party, Lincoln asserted that it should become a national party, and that it should include freed blacks, who would receive the right to vote.

End of the Civil War

At the Hampton Roads Peace Conference in February of 1865, Lincoln and Secretary of State Seward met with the vice president of the CSA, Alexander Stephens. Lincoln made a stern offer: reunion of the states, emancipation of the slaves, and immediate disbanding of the Confederate army. The Confederates, however, were not yet ready to return to the Union. The Northern General U.S. Grant then led troops toward the CSA capital at Richmond. Finally, at Appomattox (VA) in April of 1865, Lee surrendered to Grant. Soon after, the Confederate President Jefferson Davis would be caught and jailed. Finally, on April 14, 1865, Lincoln was fatally wounded by two shots from the gun of John Wilkes Booth in Ford's Theater in Washington.

Presidential Reconstruction plan

Andrew Johnson, a Jacksonian Democrat from Tennessee, became president after the assassination of Lincoln. Though a Southerner, he believed the yeoman farmers of the South had been tricked into war by "cotton snobs." Johnson's plan for reconstruction called for amnesty to be granted to all ex-Confederates except for high-ranking officials and wealthy cotton planters, who would be allowed to apply for special pardons. Johnson also called for a provisional Unionist governor to be appointed in each Southern state; this leader would hold a constitutional convention at which it would be necessary to disavow secession; repudiate the CSA debt; and accept the 13th amendment. This plan was largely a failure, however, because it infringed on the powers of Congress, was seen as too lenient on the South, threatened the Republicans by giving too much power to Southern Democrats, and ignored freed blacks, who were repressed in the South by the so-called Black Codes.

Congress' Reconstruction plan

With the Wade-Davis Bill of 1864, Congress outlined their plan for the rehabilitation of the South after the Civil War. Unlike Lincoln, who had only asked for a 10% (of 1860 voters) loyalty nucleus, Congress wanted a majority before admitting Southern states back into the Union. Participants in the state constitutional conventions would be required to sign an "ironclad oath" pledging eternal loyalty to the Union. Ex-Confederate officials would not be allowed to vote or hold office. Slavery, of course, would be abolished. Finally, the Confederate debt would be repudiated, and those who loaned money to the Confederacy would be unable to get it back. Lincoln vetoed this bill, mainly because he wanted the abolition of slavery to be an amendment rather than a law.

Tenure of Office Act

The Tenure of Office Act of 1867 established that in order to fire any Cabinet member, the president had to get the approval of the Senate. Though basically unconstitutional, this act almost ended the presidency of Johnson when he tried to dismiss Edwin Stanton, his Secretary of War. Johnson was charged with a crime, impeached by the House of Representatives, and missed being impeached by the Senate by one vote. The Supreme Court, though generally quiet during this period, made a couple of significant rulings. In ex parte Milligan (1866), the Supreme Court asserted that it is unconstitutional for military rule to continue after regular courts have been reinstated. In ex parte McCardle (1868), a similar case, the Supreme Court was actually too afraid of Congressional radicals to make a ruling.

Radical Republican Reconstruction Plan

By 1867, Johnson's Reconstruction plan had largely failed. His unwillingness to change drove many moderate congressmen to become radicals. Radical Republicans came up with their own Reconstruction plan. First, a "Joint Committee of 15" went South to explore the damage done by the war; while there, they discovered the "Black Codes" repressing freed slaves. With the Civil Rights Act of 1866, they provided basic rights for ex-slaves (not including the right to vote). The 14th amendment then gave blacks citizenship, and said that state governments could not deny anyone life, liberty and property without due process. This amendment disqualified ex-Confederates from holding public office, and declared that states could lose representation if they infringed on the rights of blacks. With the Congressional Reconstruction Act (Military Reconstruction Act) of 1867, the South was divided into 5 districts and placed under martial law; Congress forced this bill through, and eventually all of the Southern states capitulated.

Ku Klux Klan and Amnesty Act

In the 1870s, Southern whites, as members of the Conservatives or Redeemers, began to regain control of the local governments; they sought to do away with "Negro rule." The Ku Klux Klan was founded in 1867 by former Confederate General Nathan Bedford Forrest and other ex-Confederates. Though founded as a social club, this group quickly got out of hand, causing the passage of the Ku Klux Klan and Force Acts (1870-1), unsuccessful attempts to subdue the Klan by allowing for black militias. The Amnesty Act of 1872 extended the right to vote to many more ex-Confederates. Gradually, the North began to lose interest in the South for the following reasons: they were disgusted by the corrupt governments; they were frustrated by the persistent racism; and they had agreed to remain distant in exchange for a higher tariff.

Radical Republican Reconstruction Governments in the South

Carpetbaggers were those Northerners who, under the guise of reinvesting in the Southern economy, took advantage of the situation by acquiring positions in local governments and raising taxes. Scalawags were those white Republican Southerners who took similar economic advantage. During the rule of the Reconstruction governments, blacks were allowed to hold some public offices, though not if they were freed slaves; the black Senator Hiram Revels (MS) served in Jefferson Davis' old seat. Blacks had very few economic rights and had no land. Thaddeus Stevens declared that blacks should receive "40 acres and a mule," but nobody was willing to take this land from its present owners. Sharecropping became basically another form of slavery. In short, the Reconstruction governments were corrupt, spent too much and levied too many taxes, and took advantage of newly-freed slaves. Still, these governments established state constitutions, built roads and schools, and made education compulsory.

Grant administration

Graft and corruption under Grant

The Grant administration was so corrupt that the president himself had to apologize. One of the most famous fiascos of the era was the Credit Mobilier scandal: the Union Pacific gave a contract to the Credit Mobilier after the federal government secretly loaned Credit Mobilier money for their bid. Then, Vice-president Schuyler Colfax was caught accepting a bribe in return for ceasing the investigation. In the Fisk-Gould scandal, Jim Fisk and Jay Gould convinced Grant to keep government gold out of the New York Stock Exchange, because they hoped to corner the market. Grant became angry with the men and dumped $4 million worth of gold onto the market. September 24, 1869 is known as Black Friday on Wall Street; this was the day that Grant's gold flood caused the price of gold to drop so rapidly that the entire market crashed. Gould was able to survive this catastrophe; Fisk was not.

William Marcy "Boss" Tweed was the political boss of New York City. He ran the *Tammany Hall* political machine, a group that fixed elections by recruiting voters with food and jobs. Another instance of corruption under Grant was the *Congressional salary grab*: Congress voted to give themselves a 50% raise, set retroactively by two years. The public was outraged by this avarice, and so, though they kept the pay raise, Congress gave up the back pay. In the *Whiskey ring scandal*, some tax agents who were supposed to be taxing barrels of whiskey were found to have been accepting bribes; this scandal went up as high as Secretary of the Treasury Benjamin Bristow. When historians look at this period and try to figure out why there was so much corruption, they generally decide that it was a carryover from the brutality of the war, combined with the naiveté of the president.

Election of 1868

After the Civil War, the US was consumed by materialism. The election of 1868 pitted Ulysses S. Grant (Republican) against Horatio Seymour (Democrat). Grant was a war hero, and Seymour spent much of the campaign defending himself from allegations that he aided the Confederacy. The Democrats proposed that states should decide for themselves the question of black suffrage, and they wanted to give amnesty to former Confederates. Republicans had much more success with their campaign, blaming the Democrats for the war (a strategy known as "waving the bloody shirt"), and Grant won handily. Grant's presidency would not be as easy as his campaign, however. He had no political experience and was unused to compromise. He frequently fought with his Cabinet, though Secretary of State Hamilton Fish was able to convince him to sign the Treaty of Washington (1871), in which Britain compensated the US for aiding the Confederate navy.

<u>Opposition to graft and corruption</u>
Thomas Nast was one of the first famous political cartoonists; he made his name satirizing corrupt politicians like Boss Tweed. Grant established the Civil Service Commission in 1871, an organization whose mission was to study corruption and make recommendations to the president. Grant paid little attention to this group, however, and it died a quiet death in 1875. During Grant's first term, a group of upper-class Republicans, calling themselves the Mugwumps, began to call for a civil service based only on merit. At the same time, the Liberal Republicans, another splinter group of the Republican party, spoke out against the graft in civil service, the use of paper money and the Republican Reconstruction policy. This group supported a lower tariff and better treatment for farmers.

<u>Election of 1872 and the final collapse of Grant</u>
In the election of 1872, Grant won a second term (over Liberal Republican Horace Greeley) because of his enduring status as a war-hero, and because the worst scandals of his administration had yet to be exposed. Quickly, though, Grant's administration fell apart. Five Cabinet members would be found guilty of corruption. Then came the Panic of 1873. This was the result of three factors: the withdrawal of European investment (Europeans were funneling their money into the Franco-Prussian War); the stock market crash caused by the Fisk-Gould scandal; and the inflexibility of the banks caused by heavy investment in non-liquid assets. As a result of these factors, Jay Cooke and Co., one of the largest banks in the US, collapsed, taking several other banks with it. 89 railroads soon went under, and then the iron and steel mills had no business. By 1875, half a million Americans were unemployed, and farmers were beginning to lose their land to foreclosure.

Solutions to the Panic of 1873

By 1873, currency deflation was a major problem in the US. There were a number of supporters of cheap money, and they encouraged the US government to issue $26 million in greenbacks to stimulate the economy; this plan failed. There was another group of hard-money advocates who suggested using a gold standard, so the government made a compromise called the Specie Resumption Act of 1875. This act increased the number of national banks in the South and West; allowed national banks to issue as many notes as they wanted (up to a $300 million limit); and named a "day of redemption," on which all greenbacks could be exchanged for gold coins. The day of redemption never came to pass, however, which seemed to be a victory for the cheap money supporters. Instead, it became evident that the promise of gold exchange caused the public to treat greenbacks as if they were "good as gold." By 1879, the economy was back on track and the Republicans had acquired the reputation as the party in favor of business.

Rutherford B. Hayes

<u>Election of 1876 and the national self-evaluation</u>
The election of 1876, won by Rutherford B. Hayes (Republican) over Samuel J. Tilden (Democrat), coincided with the US centennial, and so people were compelled to consider

the history of the country thus far. When Americans of 1876 looked back, they had some reason to be pleased: they had survived a Civil War intact and had witnessed the end of slavery. They also had developed a strong national government. On the other hand, many Americans were disillusioned at this time by the scandals of the Grant administration. There had also been violent and disheartening struggles between black militiamen and the Ku Klux Klan in the South. Finally, many in the country were still reeling from Custer's bloody defeat at the Battle of Little Big Horn.

Industrialization, Reform, and Imperialism

New South in the 1880s

In the 1880s, the old Southern plantations began to break up, in part because the high taxes imposed by the new governments made them unprofitable. The land was mainly worked by tenant farmers and sharecroppers: tenant farmers worked and paid rent on someone else's land, while sharecroppers worked the whole plantation and got a share of the crop. Tenant farmers were mostly poor whites, while sharecroppers were mostly freed blacks. There was considerable diversification in agriculture around this time, brought on not only by innovation (cotton picker, tractor), but by the Morrill Land Grant Act, which gave grants for the creation of agricultural colleges. Clarence Birdseye's development of the refrigerated railroad car spurred farming as well. Also, as the road and rail infrastructure improved in the South, so did Southern industry.

Election of 1876 and compromise of 1877

In 1876, Rutherford B. Hayes (Republican) defeated Samuel Tilden (Democrat) after an electoral commission composed mostly of Republicans ruled that certain votes by carpet-bag governments should have gone to him. As part of the ensuing Compromise of 1877, the South was given federal money for improvements to infrastructure, a Southerner was placed in Hayes' Cabinet, and the Union troops propping up the carpetbag governments were removed. This election established the tradition of the "Solid South": it was assumed that every year the majority of Southerners would vote for the Democratic candidate.

Black Southerners and segregation

Most Southern Democrats supported *segregation*, or the separation of the races. Although the Civil Rights Act of 1875 had outlawed segregated restaurants and hotels, among other things, the Supreme Court ruled in 1883 that this act violated the 14th amendment because only states, and not individuals, could be forbidden from segregation. The Jim Crow laws were those rules that segregated blacks and whites. Although de facto (by custom) segregation had existed in the North for years, the South began to implement segregation de jure (by law). In Plessy v. Ferguson (1896), the Supreme Court ruled that accommodations should be "separate but equal." In Cummings v. Board of Education (1898), the Supreme Court allowed public schools to be segregated.

Redeemers

The *Redeemers* sought to prevent blacks from voting and to return power to the "natural leaders." In response, the Populist party was formed; it was an uneasy alliance of blacks and poor whites. Southern Democrats tried to exploit the tension within the Populist party. In order to keep blacks from voting, Democrats subjected voters to literacy tests, property tests, criminal background checks, residency requirements and the so-called Grandfather Clause, which stated that individuals could not vote unless their ancestors had voted before January 1, 1867. These restrictions, known collectively as the Mississippi Plan, were actually upheld by the Supreme Court, which ruled in Williams v. Mississippi (1898) that they were legal because they never explicitly stated that blacks could not vote.

Booker T. Washington and W.E.B. DuBois

Booker T. Washington was an ex-slave who founded the Tuskegee Institute; he felt that blacks should establish economic independence before worrying about political rights. In his Atlanta Exposition speech, he declared that blacks needed to humble themselves to whites. Professor W.E.B. DuBois attacked Washington's speech as a compromise; DuBois believed blacks should take everything they were due. In 1914, both Washington and DuBois met with Marcus Garvey, who believed that blacks should return to Africa and establish a separate country (interestingly, most of Garvey's financial support came from the KKK). At around this time, Paul Laurence Dunbar was achieving renown as the "poet laureate of the Negro race," and Charles Waddell Chestnut was admired as a popular black novelist.

Native Americans

Solutions to the Indian Problem
The US government constructed several policies in an attempt to solve the so-called "Indian Problem." The Dawes (Severalty) Act of 1887 asserted that Natives needed to be assimilated into American society; tribes were moved onto "allotments of severalty" (reservations), which they supposedly owned, although they had no control of the land. The Indian Reorganization (Howard-Wheeler) Act of 1934 encouraged a return to tribal life, and offered Natives money for college. In 1953, with the so-called "termination policy," Natives became the responsibility of the states rather than the federal government. In 1970, the new strategy was "self-determination without termination": Natives were allowed to move where they choose, and were promised money (which they did not receive).

Subordination of the western Native Americans Until 1874
The Native Americans who roamed the Great Plains were known as fierce hunters and there were a few bloody encounters between settlers heading west and the natives. In 1851, the US established the Concentration policy, which encouraged Native Americans to live close to one another. This strategy was untenable, however, and the period from 1860-90 was marked by frequent conflict. In the Sioux Wars of 1865-7, the Sioux were led by Red Cloud; they fought and lost to American troops after their sacred hunting ground was mined. For a while, the US tried to group tribes on reservations in Oklahoma and the Black Hills; from 1869-74, Generals Sherman and Sheridan engaged in a War of Extermination to kill those who refused to move.

Subordination of the western Native Americans from 1875-1887
According to Grant's Peace Program, each Native American tribe would be put under the control of different religious groups. In 1875, miners were allowed back into the Black Hills, prompting the Sioux War of 1875-6, during which Sitting Bull defeated Custer at the Battle of Little Big Horn. Around this time, Chief Joseph attempted to lead his Nez Perce tribe to Canada; this mission failed and the Nez Perce were sent to Oklahoma. The Apache leader Geronimo was defeated in Arizona in 1887. At the Battle of Wounded Knee, the US army massacred 300, mostly women and children. Native Americans were doomed by their inferior weapons; by the destruction by whites of their food supply, the buffalo; and by railroads which made it easier for whites to encroach on their hunting grounds.

Spanish-American War

The Spanish-American War only lasted between six and eight weeks before the US claimed victory. The first phase of it was fought in the Philippines, and the second in Cuba. In Cuba, the United States scored a crucial victory when a rag-tag group of soldiers known as the Roughriders (Theodore Roosevelt among them) took Kettle Hill and secured Santiago. Although the Teller Amendment of 1898 had promised independence to Cuba after the war, the Platt Amendment, which was inserted into the Cuban Constitution in 1901, made Cuba a protectorate of the US. The US control of Guantanamo Bay dates back to this amendment. In 1934, Cuba received its independence. The Spanish-American War formally ended with the signing of the Treaty of Paris in 1898. The US received Guam, the Philippines, Puerto Rico, Cuba, and Wake Island. The US also paid the Spanish $20 million because Manila had supposedly surrendered after the end of the war, making it an invalid wartime concession.

Causes of the Spanish-American War
The Spanish-American War centered around Cuba. There had already been several revolts against the Spanish leadership on that island, and the Wilson-Gorman Tariff had damaged the Cuban economy. In 1896, the Spanish sent General Valeriano Weyler to establish a reconcentration camp, where the dissenting Cubans could be weeded out. Many in the United States pushed the government to intervene in Cuba; businessmen were worried about their crops, Christians and humanitarians were worried about the Cuban people, and imperialists saw a good chance to seize the island. The two final causes of the war were the DeLome letter, in which the Spanish minister to the US insulted President McKinley, and the explosion of the USS Maine in Havana Harbor. Although the Spanish still claim to not have caused this explosion, the US nevertheless declared war on April 25, 1898.

John Hay's defense of China

From 1898 to 1905, John Hay was the Secretary of State. One of his great achievements was establishing the Open Door Policy with respect to China. China had just been defeated by Japan and was in the process of being carved up by the European powers into various spheres of economic influence. Hay asserted that each nation should allow equal access for all nations and should respect the rights of the Chinese. Somewhat surprisingly, Europe agreed to this policy of goodwill. The Open Door Policy did not, however, keep China from being exploited by foreign traders. In the Boxer Rebellion of 1900, the Chinese rose up against foreigners and were promptly routed by an international coalition (including the US).

Debate over the Philippines and the Filipino War

In the years 1898 and 1899, the question of what to do about the Philippines was hotly debated in the US. Imperialists (including Henry Cabot Lodge and Theodore Roosevelt), wanted to make the group of islands into a state, argued against Anti-imperialists (e.g., Andrew Carnegie, Mark Twain) who felt that the US would be drawn into Asian conflicts. Some politicians, like William Jennings Bryan, voted for the Treaty of Paris and the acquisition of the Philippines because they felt it would be a disaster that would discourage further imperialism. In 1899, the Filipino leader Aguinaldo led the people against US forces. This uprising was only crushed after much cruelty. Later, the Tydings-McDuffie Act of 1934 promised independence to the Philippines within 10 years but they did not receive it until 1946. Some relevant Supreme Court rulings from this period were in the Insular Cases of

1901: the Court asserted that citizens of US territories do not have the same rights as citizens of the continental US.

Theodore Roosevelt

Beginnings of the Panama Canal
The Spanish-American War had demonstrated that the US needed a Latin American canal in order to become a major naval power. At that time, however, their hands were tied by the Clayton-Bulwer Treaty of 1850, which had stated that neither the US nor Britain would build a canal in Latin America without the other. Fortunately for the US, the British were distracted by the Boer War in South Africa and thus were willing to sign the Hay-Pauncefote Treaty in 1901, allowing the US to go it alone. Many in the US, including Roosevelt, wanted to build the canal in Nicaragua because it has a number of lakes that could be connected, and because it is mostly flat. Others lobbied for Panama, pointing out that a French contractor had already started work on a canal there and that Panama was narrower than Nicaragua.

Organization required prior to building the Panama Canal
In 1902, the United States struck a deal with a Panamanian builder for the control of the canal project. The US then needed to acquire the land. Panama at this time was owned by Colombia; the Colombians rejected the first offer made by the US, leading Roosevelt to call them "blackmailers." Then, in 1903, a rebellion broke out in Panama; Roosevelt recognized the new, independent country after less than a day of fighting. 15 days later, the US purchased the Panama Canal Zone from the new foreign minister for $10 million initially and $250,000 per year. Many observers were embarrassed by the deal the United States had won from a fledgling country. Nevertheless, Roosevelt then hired engineer John Stephens to finish the job.

Building and opening of the Panama Canal
Once Roosevelt finally secured the building supplies and the land to construct the Panama Canal, the brutal and dangerous work began. In order to prevent malaria the US paved streets, drained swamps, and built houses so that the workers would not have to sleep in tents. Nevertheless, the workdays were long and the pay was low. In the end, the canal cost about $400 million; it was finished in 1913, but did not open until the next year. Roosevelt's visit to Panama made him the first president to leave the US during his term. In 1920, a guilty Democratic Congress gave Colombia $25 million. At present, about 12,000 ships go through the canal every year and it takes about 8 hours to get from one end to the other.

Second Hague Disarmament Conference and Treaty of Portsmouth
At the *Second Hague Disarmament Conference* in 1907, a number of nations gathered to reaffirm the Hague Conference rules of humane warfare and agreed upon how the collection of debts should be pursued. After the Russo-Japanese War, Roosevelt rather reluctantly agreed to mediate between the two countries. The result was the *Treaty of Portsmouth*, in which the defeated Japanese lost some land (though not as much as the Russians felt was appropriate). For this, Roosevelt received the 1906 Nobel Peace Prize. After the Russo-Japanese War, many Japanese workers came to the US; Roosevelt had to intervene and prevent them from being discriminated against. Finally, Roosevelt promoted the US Navy by painting a number of ships white and parading them past the Asian coast.

Roosevelt and the 2nd Venezuelan Crisis

In 1902, many Latin American countries were deep in debt to Europe and were not making any moves to repay their debts. Enraged, European countries began to use military force. At first, Roosevelt supported this policy, but he gradually changed his mind, in part because the American public was opposed to it. When Germany, therefore, sent ships to Santo Domingo in 1904, Roosevelt announced the Roosevelt Corollary to the Monroe Doctrine: this document stated that nations may not use force to collect debts. Roosevelt asserted that the US would peaceably arbitrate these disputes before Europe could get violent; he felt these interventions would help Latin America and prevent European recolonization. The US developed a reputation as "the policeman of the Caribbean."

William Howard Taft

Foreign policy of Taft

Roosevelt was succeeded in the White House by William Howard Taft, who became known for "dollar diplomacy"; the United States would loan money to Latin American countries so that these countries could pay off their European debts. The US would also dabble a bit in Latin American politics, trying to influence the governments for the benefit of American business. The Taft administration also wanted to encourage trade with China and therefore helped prop up some American banking interests there. Taft is also known for his association with the creation of the World Court. The US, Britain, and France tried to establish an international judiciary. This idea enraged former president Roosevelt; he preferred settling differences on the battlefield.

Homestead Act of 1862 and the Transcontinental Railroad

The US government tried many different ways to improve conditions for farmers in the West. Under the Homestead Act of 1862, farmers were sold 160 acres for $10, with the proviso that they had to improve the land within 5 years. Between the years 1865 and 1900, only one in six farms began this way. The Timber Culture Act of 1873 gave more land to farmers, with the proviso that they had to plant some trees on that land. One thing that helped to populate the West was the completion of the Transcontinental Railroad in 1869. The Union Pacific met the Central Pacific railway at Promontory Point, Utah. In 1889, the US government opened Oklahoma for settlement, and by 1893 it was completely settled.

Era of bonanzas

Between the years 1848 and 1858, the miners known as the "forty-niners" dug about $555 million out of the Western soil. In particular, the Comstock Lode of Virginia City, Nevada was famous for producing vast amounts of gold and silver. After buffalo were largely eradicated from the Great Plains, there was a "cattleman's bonanza," aided by the invention of barbed wire. The Cattleman's Association was a union of cattle dealers joined together to preserve the integrity of the industry, to stop cross-breeding, and to stop cattle thievery. This era marked the end of the open range, mainly because of horrible droughts and bad winters, range wars between the cowboys and sheep farmers, the railroads and barbed wire.

Industrial era scandals and innovations

The infamous Credit Mobilier scandal occurred during Grant's presidency and involved the Union Pacific Railroad. A more egregious crime was perpetrated on the stockholders of the Erie Railroad; the owners were trying to avoid being bought out by Vanderbilt, and thus they printed up a huge amount of new stock, making it impossible for Vanderbilt to get a majority interest but also vastly diminishing the value of each share. During this era, the following innovations and inventors accelerated industry: sleeper cars (George Pullman); air brakes for trains (George Westinghouse); time zones; double tracking (so that two trains could run on the same line); and the standardization of the distance from one rail to another,

Second Industrial Revolution

The Second Industrial Revolution was possible in the United States because of the abundance of raw materials and the laissez-faire economic policies of the government. In the space between the years 1860 and 1914, industry grew to about twelve times its original size. This rapid progress was made possible by the rapid growth of the American railway system. The railroads were subsidized by the federal government. Around this time, Samuel Morse developed his telegraph code, enabling almost instantaneous communication across vast distances. Jay Gould and James J. Hill were among those who made immense fortunes as railroad managers. Cornelius Vanderbilt and his son William were both railroad magnates with a reputation for ignoring the plight of their workers.

J.P. Morgan and banker control

The Panic of 1893 was brought on by the collapse of the Philadelphia and Reading Railroads; soon after, 192 railroads failed. In a panic, railroad magnates turned to bankers, especially the "Railroad Doctor," J.P. Morgan. Morgan insisted that all of the business' records be opened to him. His usual strategy was to encourage old investors to reinvest, to sell more, "watered-down" stock, and to place either himself or one of his associates on the Board of Directors. In this way, Morgan was able to create a set of "interlocking directories," conglomerations of businesses in which he had an interest. He created many large companies this way, among them General Electric, Western Union, and Equitable.

Competition and disorder in the industrial era

The late eighteenth century was marked by intense competition between the railroads. Railroads offered secret illegal refunds to big customers and in areas where they had no competition, they charged exorbitant prices. After the 1870s, various states tried to tame the railroads; one such instance of this kind of regulation was the Granger Laws. Farmers often felt that they were charged more than others. In Munn v. Illinois (1877), the Supreme Court asserted that the state governments had the right to regulate the railroads. In Wabash, St. Louis, and Pacific Railroad Co. v. Illinois (1886), the Supreme Court reversed its former opinion and declared that only the federal government could regulate the railroads. Finally, with the Interstate Commerce Act of 1887, the federal government forbade discriminatory practices like refunds and price fixing; unfortunately, these laws were rarely enforced.

John D. Rockefeller and the trust

John D. Rockefeller came from a working-class background, but gradually rose to become the owner of the wildly profitable Standard Oil company. Rockefeller was known for spying on his competitors and intimidating his employees. In 1870, Standard allied itself with 40 other companies; when this alliance began, the group controlled 10% of the market, but by 1881 they controlled almost 95%. In 1882, Standard Oil created a trust: alliance members gave their stock to Standard in exchange for trust certificates. The federal government began to get suspicious of these powerful trusts, and in 1890 the Sherman Anti-trust Act was passed. This act forbade trusts, but it was worded so vaguely that it was ineffective. In the case of US v. E.C. Knight Co. (1895), the Supreme Court ruled that the Knight sugar refinery was not a monopoly because it didn't hurt interstate trade; businesses saw this ruling as a call to monopolize.

Andrew Carnegie and steel

The potential for making money in steel was made possible by the development of the Bessemer process, whereby iron ore was converted into wrought iron and then has its impurities removed with cold air. Andrew Carnegie, an immigrant from Scotland who rose to the top of the Pennsylvania Railroad, was one of the first to make his fortune in steel. He was not especially knowledgeable about steel, but he was the first manager to make a point of vertical integration: that is, control of every step of the production process. Carnegie bought out most of his competitors, until he was eventually bought out by J.P. Morgan. Carnegie and his fellows believed in a sort of "gospel of wealth," the idea that they had risen to the top through a process like natural selection. They also believed in using their money for the community.

Gilded Age

Social critics and dissenters in the Gilded Age
In his book Dynamic Sociology, Lester Frank Ward railed against the Social Darwinism espoused by the upper class; he declared that humans were more than mere animals. In Progress and Poverty, Henry George asserted that poverty was the result of poor legislation rather than any inherent weakness in the poor. Edward Bellamy promoted socialism in his novel Looking Back (1888); in it, a man of the year 2000 describes how America was turned into a utopian society through the abolition of corporations. Also at this time, Thorstein Veblen exposed the phenomenon of "conspicuous consumption" in his Theory of the Leisure Class. All of these critics were disgusted by the hypocrisy of the robber barons; these magnates claimed to support laissez-faire government, yet they wanted high tariffs to protect their businesses.

Laissez-faire conservatism and the gospel of wealth
The so-called "Gilded Age" of American history, which ran roughly from 1880 to 1900, only looked prosperous from a distance. Many at this time believed that wealth justified itself, and that God showed his favor in people by making them rich. Many business leaders did not trust politicians because they did not feel that they had had to fight their way to the top. Businessmen believed that the role of the government was to protect property and trade through tariffs. William Graham Sumner wrote the essay "What the Social Classes Owe Each Other," in which he declared that corporations shouldn't demand high tariff rates, but the government shouldn't respond to requests to clean up the slums. There was a general sense

- 44 -

that the poor were responsible for their plight. Around this time, the popular imagination was inspired by the rags-to-riches fables of Horatio Alger.

American labor in the Gilded Age
As the US emerged from the Civil War, one of the main economic problems was that most workers were unskilled. In general, working conditions were horrendous and wages were low. There was little homogeneity in the labor force, either, making it difficult for workers to switch jobs. Immigrants were usually willing to take more dangerous jobs than natives; during the 1880s, more than 5 million immigrants entered the US. In 1882, the Chinese Exclusion Act put a 10-year moratorium on Chinese immigration. In 1885, the Foran Act prohibited American business men from traveling to China to recruit workers. Both of these acts were open violations of the Burlingame Treaty of 1868, which had provided for open Chinese immigration.

Characteristics of the Gilded Age
The period in American history between Reconstruction and the Progressive Era is commonly known as the Gilded Age. During this period, the US seemed to be simultaneously abandoning the ideals of the past and failing to anticipate the future; this was in large part due to the confusion of a horrendous Civil War and massive immigration, industrialization, and urbanization. During this period, many Americans sought refuge in community organizations like the Moose Lodge, the Elks Club, and the Masonic Lodge. The politicians of the Gilded Age tended to avoid the major issues of social injustice and inequality, instead focusing on minor issues like public v. parochial schools, and the blue laws (laws restricting commercial activity on Sunday).

Politics in the Gilded Age
Although the Republicans dominated the executive branch during the Gilded Age, Congress was evenly divided. The Republican party was composed mainly of people from the Northeast and Midwest. Blacks typically were Republicans (that is, when they were allowed into the political process). In general, the Republicans supported high tariffs and sound money. One of the main internal disputes in the Republican party was between the stalwarts, who supported the spoils system, and the half-breeds, who did not. As for the Democrats, they were largely based in the South or in the big cities of the North. The Democrats and Republicans butted heads over ethnic, religious, and cultural issues, but they tended to avoid larger economic and social issues. Extremely talented individuals were more likely to go into business than politics during this era. Another trend of the Gilded Age was the domination of the president by Congress.

Labor organizations after the Civil War

At the end of the Civil War, only about 2% of all US workers were unionized; many believed joining a union was an admission that one would never move up. Over time, though, people began to realize that the consolidation of business interests (trusts) had to be met by a consolidation of labor. In 1866, the *National Labor Union* was founded by William H. Sylvis; this idealistic organization advocated an 8-hour work day but disbanded after backing the loser in the 1872 election. In 1869, Uriah Stephens founded the *Noble and Holy Orders of the Knights of Labor*; this group excluded doctors, lawyers, and bankers and supported the end of sexism; the 8-hour workday; paper money; income tax; and the prohibition of alcohol.

Great Strike of 1877, Homestead Strike, and Pullman Strike

The *Great Strike of 1877* occurred in West Virginia when state police and militiamen were sent to break up a railway strike and joined it instead. President Hayes sent in the army and at least 100 people were killed breaking up the strike. This debacle set a bad precedent for future strikes. In the *Homestead (PA) Strike* of July 1892, a group of soldiers called by Henry Clay Frick (temporarily in charge of one of Carnegie's steel mills) brutally broke up a strike. In 1894, a group of Pullman railcar employees began a strike, supported by the American Railway Union of Eugene V. Debs. All rail workers then went on strike out of sympathy for the Pullman workers. The rail owners got an injunction, claiming that the rail workers were interfering with interstate trade and therefore violating the Sherman Anti-trust Act. This did not end the strike, and thus President Grover Cleveland had to send in the army under the false premise that the strike was holding up the US mail.

Labor organizations after the Civil War

In 1886, the Knights of Labor gathered in *Haymarket Square* in Chicago to protest an attack against another union. During the protest, a bomb was thrown and several people were killed; 7 members of the union were arrested, and some were executed. This incident linked labor unions with violence in the popular imagination. At the same time, less idealistic labor unions like the American Railway Union (led by Eugene V. Debs), the United Mineworkers, and the Molly McGuires were making great inroads in working communities. The *American Federation of Labor* was an alliance of many unions formed in 1881. This group sought a shorter workday, better working conditions, and workman's compensation: they were also not afraid to strike. The AFL frequently engaged in collective bargaining, in which a strike was threatened in order to bring management to the negotiation table.

Opposition to organized labor

The general public opposed labor unions because they disliked the idea of closed shops (those places in which one had to be a union member to work) and because they had a reputation for violence. Unions were also fiercely competitive with one another, and there was some animosity between the unions for skilled and unskilled workers. Unions were always at a disadvantage in their dealings with management, in part because management could hire lobbyists (to promote anti-union legislation in Washington) and lawyers, and could bribe politicians. Owners often had blacklists of union trouble-makers who would not be hired, and plenty of "yellow-dog" workers who had signed contracts pledging never to join a union. Owners often hired spies to obtain information among workers, and, in the event of strike, they could always hire "scabs" to cross the picket lines. It was not unheard of for managers to hire thugs to cause trouble among strikers and perpetuate the rowdy reputation of the unions.

Highlights of the Hayes presidency

Foolishly, Rutherford B. Hayes made himself a lame-duck president by announcing soon after taking office that he would not seek a second term. Hayes' wife was nicknamed "Lemonade Lucy," because she would not allow any alcohol in the White House. Hayes tried to restore the power of the presidency after the debacle of Grant, but he was weakened by intense struggles over his Cabinet confirmations. One thing Hayes can be credited with is making a gallant attempt to destroy the spoils system. He replaced the Collector of the

Customs House after discovering the corruption of that body, and he appointed Carl Schurz Secretary of the Interior on the basis of merit. In turn, Schurz established a merit system in his department, creating an entrance exam for potential employees.

Hayes vs. Greenbackers and the Silverites

After the Specie Resumption Act of 1875, Hayes worked to minimize the effects of the oncoming "day of redemption," in which paper money could be exchanged for gold coins. He began a policy of contraction, wherein the government gradually took in paper money and issued gold, and he funded attempts to mine more gold. The Greenbackers were those who wanted Hayes to postpone the day of redemption; he did not, and it ultimately proved anticlimactic, as people assumed their paper money was "good as gold" and didn't bother to redeem it. Hayes also had to deal with the Silverites. In 1873, the government had enraged silver prospectors by announcing that it would no longer make coins out of silver. In answer to their fury, Hayes pushed through the Bland-Allison Act, which established that a minimum of $2 million of silver had to be purchased and coined by the government every month.

Lowpoints of the Hayes presidency

One of the failures of the Hayes administration was its handling of the Great Rail Strike of 1877. When over two-thirds of the rail lines were shut down by strikes, Hayes sent in federal troops, and there was considerable bloodshed. This set a bad precedent for how strikes would be handled in the future. Hayes vetoed an attempt by western labor unions to restrict Chinese immigration, saying that this would be a violation of the Burlingame Treaty. One of the main issues in the Hayes years was monetary policy. Farmers, who were often in debt, wanted a soft currency not backed by anything; they were willing to settle for a silver standard. In Hepburn v. Griswold (1869), the Supreme Court had ruled that there could not be paper money without a gold standard; in the Legal Tender cases of 1871, however, the Court reversed itself. The bickering over these conflicting rulings plagued the Hayes administration.

Grover Cleveland

In 1884, the incumbent Arthur was passed over by his party in favor of Secretary of State James G. Blaine. This proved to be a bad move, as the Democratic candidate, Grover Cleveland, was able to win the support of conservative Republicans (Mugwumps) and claim a narrow victory. The highlights of the Cleveland administration include the further reform of civil service and the government's successful stand against ex-Union soldiers who were protesting for large pensions. Cleveland reluctantly signed the Interstate Commerce Act, and he was correct in predicting that it would not be enforced. Cleveland also spent a great deal of time on tariffs: he attempted to reduce the overall duty with the Mongrel Tariff and the Mills Bill of 1888, neither of which were very successful.

Benjamin Harrison in the election of 1888

In 1888, the Republican Benjamin Harrison narrowly upset the incumbent Cleveland, despite having less of the popular vote. Harrison did not accomplish much civil service reform, and spent a great deal of time managing insubordination in Congress. Harrison's Republican agenda promoted the Federal Election Bill, which was a response to the Mississippi Plan designed to protect the voting rights of freedmen. The Silver Purchase Bill was favored by the west, but lacked the votes to get through. In the Compromise of 1890, the Western Republicans got the silver purchase (Sherman Silver Purchase Act), Southern

Democrats got the defeat of the Federal Election Bill, and the Northern Republicans got a higher tariff (McKinley Tariff of 1890). Harrison's administration became known for giving money away for virtually any reason: pensions were excessive; the silver purchase cost federal money; and all of the income tax taken during the Civil War was given back to the people.

Election of 1892 and the panic of 1893

Grover Cleveland (Dem) defeated Benjamin Harrison (Rep) in the election of 1892 primarily because of his financial conservatism, his promise to change the tariff and because the epidemic of strikes in 1892 had weakened Harrison. Then came the Panic of 1893, caused by labor troubles, overspeculation in the railroads, and an agricultural depression. First the Philadelphia and Reading Railroads collapsed, then the stock markets collapsed, then the banks folded, draining the gold reserves, then the other railroads folded, and finally the factories were forced to close. Cleveland believed that the cause of this Panic was the Sherman Silver Purchase Act, so he repealed it. This plan did absolutely nothing financially, and it split the Democratic party politically.

James A. Garfield

Garfield and Arthur in the election of 1880

In the election of 1880, the Republican party was beset by internal squabbling between the stalwarts and half-breeds over the issue of patronage. This led to a chaotic nominating convention in which a campaign manager, James A. Garfield, became the candidate. Garfield won a narrow victory over the Democrat Winfield Scott Hancock, a war hero with no political experience. Garfield was a charismatic figure whose administration began with a successful compromise among Republicans; unfortunately, he was shot and killed in 1881. Garfield was succeeded by his vice-president, Chester A. Arthur. The major event of his presidency was the Civil Service Act of 1883, which established a commission to create competitive examinations for potential government employees. Arthur also helped create the modern US navy.

Panic of 1893 and the domestic affairs under Cleveland

After the Panic of 1893, a group known as the Silverite school declared that the economic problems could be solved if the US would begin coining silver again. Cleveland, however, ignored this advice, and elected to buy gold with the profits from the sale of government bonds. This strategy was somewhat successful. It was during the Panic of 1893 that the suggestion to battle economic depression by employing people on public works was first made. One of Cleveland's major policy moves in his second term was the Wilson-Gorman Tariff of 1894. This lowered the tariff rate and established trade with Latin America. It also established a small income tax on wealthy individuals, though this income tax would be repealed in the Supreme Court case Pollock v. Farmer's Loan and Trust (1895). Cleveland's last term was diminished by ineffective enforcement of the Sherman Anti-trust Act and the Interstate Commerce Act.

Populism

Problems during Populism

In the years following the Civil War, the US heartland suffered from an overabundance of wheat and rice; these surpluses, coupled with the advances in transportation and communication, drove prices down. Farmers were forced into high debt which they could never repay, leading to deflation and a scarcity of currency. Since many farmers didn't own the land that they worked, the banks often had to foreclose when farmers were unable to pay their debts. Farmers blamed their problems on a number of different factors. They blamed the railroads, which usually gave discount rates to bigger shippers. They blamed the banks, who loaned money to the rich but were unforgiving of farmers' economic plight. They also blamed the tax system, claiming that it was easy for businesses to hide their assets and impossible for farmers to do so. Additionally, they blamed the tariff, which discouraged other countries from buying US goods.

Early farm organization during Populism
The Patron of Husbandry (Grange) was founded in 1867 by Oliver Kelley to establish cooperatives, in which individuals bought goods directly from the whole-sale distributor. His group was also responsible for the Granger Laws, which attacked railroad and grain elevator interests. The Grange had basically disappeared by 1875. The National Farmer's Alliance and Industrial Union pursued a number of different initiatives: more national banks; cooperatives; a federal storage system for non-perishable items; more currency; free coinage of silver; reduction of tariffs; direct election of senators; an 8-hour workday; government control of railroads and telegraphs; and one term for the president. This group's success led to the formation of the Populist Party in 1890. This party aimed to speak for the farmers and included all of the farmers' unions as well as some labor unions, the Greenbackers, and the Prohibitionists. The party suffered from internal divisions from its inception.

Republican Ascendancy in the election of 1896

The Republicans had been successful in the Congressional elections of 1894, and they nominated William McKinley for president in 1896. McKinley was in favor of high tariffs and the gold standard. He was opposed by William Jennings Bryan of the Democrats. McKinley had a wealth of political experience and money, and the Democrats were blamed by many for the economic depression under Cleveland: McKinley won fairly easily. This election marked a 36-year period of domination by the Republicans. It also spelled the end of the Populist party. Around this time, gold was found in the Yukon, lending credence to the Republican belief in the gold standard.

Imperialism

Imperialism during the period of withdrawal (Civil War to 1880s)
In the period after the Civil War, the US for the most part withdrew from foreign affairs. The Secretaries of State in this period, however, were very aggressive: Seward interfered in Korean politics, tried to assert influence in the Caribbean, and famously purchased Alaska from Russia in 1867 for $7.2 million. Hamilton Fish tried and failed to annex Santo Domingo. Aside from these instances, though, the US kept its distance. For the most part, this was because it was preoccupied with its own problems. There was also a common belief that invading and colonizing other countries would be a violation of our own Declaration of Independence. Many were remembering Washington's farewell address, in which he advised the US to avoid military entanglements, and others were wary of violating the Monroe Doctrine.

<u>Imperialism during the New Manifest Destiny (1880s to 1920s)</u>
In the 1880s, the US began to take a stronger interest in foreign affairs. This was in part due to humanitarian concern: the US felt it could improve the standard of living around the world. There was also, of course, an economic motive; manufacturers wanted to find a new source of raw materials, as well as a new market for their products. Missionaries began to travel abroad in this period, trying to convert foreigners to Christianity. There were also military reasons for the increased activity abroad; the US decided it would be a good idea to acquire naval bases in the Pacific and a group known as the Jingoists openly looked for a military conflict. Theodore Roosevelt and Henry Cabot Lodge were both Jingoists.

Between the years 1889 and 1891, the US came into conflict with Italy after members of the Sicilian Black Hand, a terrorist group, were lynched without just cause in New Orleans. The US also sparred with Chile after 2 sailors from the USS Baltimore died during a bar fight in Valparaiso, Chile. At around this time, a boundary dispute erupted between British Guiana and Venezuela after gold was discovered in the vaguely-defined border region. Britain was ready to send troops into South America but the US dissuaded them from doing so, citing the Monroe Doctrine. Meanwhile, all throughout the nineteenth century the US had been closing in on a conquest of Hawaii. After New England missionaries stumbled upon the islands, the US had gotten the natives to sign trade treaties with various US companies. In the 1890s the US army, led by pineapple magnate Sanford Dole, ousted the native leadership. Hawaii was annexed by the US in 1898.

The "Seal Battle" was fought in the Bering Sea between British Canada and the US mainly over boundary lines. In 1893, the two sides met and established mutual boundaries between Alaska and Canada. In 1889, the first meeting of the Pan-American Union was held in Washington, DC. In 1878, the US had established a naval base at Pago Pago. Both the British and Germans demanded access to the base. In 1889, the US allowed both the British and Germans to jointly occupy the base. In 1899, the Samoan islands were divided up among the US and the European powers.

Theodore Roosevelt

<u>Election of 1900 and Theodore Roosevelt</u>
In the election of 1900 McKinley and Theodore Roosevelt of the Republicans defeated William Jennings Bryan of the Democrats. McKinley was then assassinated on September 6, 1901, and Roosevelt took over. Roosevelt is known as a follower of the African proverb, "Walk softly and carry a big stick." He was known for having very little respect for the system of checks and balances: if the Constitution were too rigid on an issue for his tastes, he ignored it; if Congress acted up, he would subdue them with a mixture of compromise and coercion. Roosevelt displayed his blunt skill in diplomacy in the Alaska Panhandle dispute of 1903 (in which he decided which islands the US would get, and which would belong to the British) and in the Morocco Dispute of 1905, in which he (along with Britain and France) dissuaded Germany from trying to take the North African country.

<u>Roosevelt Republicans</u>
For Roosevelt Republicans, the principles of good domestic policy could be summed up as the "3 Cs": control of the corporations; consumer protection; and the conservation of natural resources. Roosevelt had made his name as a member of the Roughriders in the Spanish-American War. Interestingly, his presidency was a result of his unpopularity in his own party: his fellow Republicans had nominated him as vice-president because this was

felt to be a weak position. They were of course quite displeased when McKinley was assassinated and Roosevelt became president. Roosevelt quickly became famous for his attacks on the trusts. He went after the Northern Securities Company, run by, among others, J.P. Morgan and John D. Rockefeller. Morgan attempted to bribe Attorney General Philip Knox to halt the investigation; Knox promptly reported this to Roosevelt. In all, 44 anti-trust cases were heard during Roosevelt's presidency.

Election of 1904
In the election of 1904, Roosevelt used the Square Deal as his platform, and was able to defeat the Democrat Judge Alton B. Parker. As part of the Square Deal, Roosevelt mandated an open shop policy; workers would be free to join a union without being obliged to do so. A case in which Roosevelt's government did not benefit workers was the Danbury Hatters' Strike. During this dispute, the workers organized a general boycott of Danbury Hats. The management argued that this boycott violated the Sherman Anti-trust Act and the Interstate Commerce Act, and the Supreme Court agreed. Many workers blamed Roosevelt for this decision.

Roosevelt's Square Deal
Roosevelt's Square Deal was a domestic agenda designed to help the working class and diminish the power of the corporations. The Elkins Act made railroad rebates illegal, making it difficult for preferential treatment to be given to corporations. Roosevelt formed the Department of Commerce and Labor to help workers. One telling episode was the Anthracite Coal Strike in 1902. When the owner of the mines asked Roosevelt for an injunction forcing the employees back to work, Roosevelt instead sent troops in to mine the coal for the government! The owner and the labor leader then met at the White House to settle their differences. This was the first time both sides in a strike had accepted an executive commission, and the first time the president had threatened to seize property. It was also the first time a president had sided with a labor union.

New programs and the Old Guard Republicans
Many Old Guard Republicans disagreed with Theodore Roosevelt on the issue of resource conservation. The Newlands Reclamation Act of 1902 tried to reclaim the wilderness through the construction of dams. Roosevelt believed that the United States only had about a quarter of its original trees; this act set aside land in the Grand Canyon, Yosemite and Yellowstone for the preservation of forests. Roosevelt also had to endure the Panic of 1907 caused by too much supply, a decrease in demand, and a short money supply resulting from a lack of gold. The Aldrich-Vreeland Act of 1908 authorized national banks to issue emergency currency. Over time, it seemed that Roosevelt had become more radical. The Employers Liability Act of 1906, for instance, had provided for workman's compensation but was struck down by the courts. Roosevelt promptly went after the courts.

Roosevelt's reforms
The Hepburn Act of 1906 gave the ICC the authority to set shipping prices in the event that a shipper complained about the rates. This act also allowed the government to regulate pipelines and express and sleeping car companies. The Pure Food and Drug Act of 1906 established the Food and Drug Administration to regulate what had become a very corrupt industry. The Meat Inspection Act of 1906 was inspired by Upton Sinclair's novel The Jungle, which exposed the corruption of the meatpacking industry. It established tougher regulation of meat handlers. Not all of Roosevelt's legislation passed, however. He was unable to pass laws against child labor, establish a national worker's compensation, or

restrict the power of the National Association of Manufacturers to gain injunctions against strikers.

Roosevelt's legacy and the election of 1908
Theodore Roosevelt, like Andrew Jackson, was truly a public servant. Most of his domestic policies really seemed aimed at improving the lot of the common American. During his administration, Roosevelt greatly enlarged the powers of the president. He created the national parks system and gave the Progressive Movement some respectability. In the 1908 election, Roosevelt chose William Howard Taft to become his successor. Roosevelt felt confident that Taft would carry on the mission of the Progressives. Taft ran against William Jennings Bryan of the Democrats, a veteran leader who favored a lower tariff and limited injunctions against strikers. Taft won the election, primarily because of his association with Roosevelt.

Taft presidency

Taft was a very cautious president. His administration saw the deepening of the gradual split between Progressive and Old Guard Republicans. Though Roosevelt had promoted him as a Progressive, Taft slowly began to act more like a member of the Old Guard. These tensions came to a head over the tariff in 1909. The Old Guard wanted to keep the tariff as it was, while Progressives fought for reductions. After the House and Senate came up with conflicting tariff bills, Taft was able to engineer a compromise; the Payne-Aldrich Act of 1909 brought the tariff down to 40.8%. This act also contained a corporate tax and the promise of an income tax in the future.

1912 election and the legacy of Taft
At the Republican convention before the election of 1912, the incumbent Taft was nominated even though Theodore Roosevelt had won most of the primaries. Enraged, Roosevelt left the Republicans and formed the Progressive (Bull-Moose) party. Roosevelt ran on his platform of New Nationalism: voting rights for women and a ban on child labor were among the initiatives. On October 14, 1912, Roosevelt was shot in the torso during a speech; he finished the speech. The election came down to a contest between Roosevelt and Woodrow Wilson of the Democrats. These two candidates had similar views on a number of issues, but while Roosevelt was willing to allow some trusts, Wilson wanted to eliminate trusts across the board. Wilson ended up winning a rather comfortable victory. As the Taft presidency came to a close, most observers saw his greatest accomplishments as the "rule of reason," in which the judiciary was allowed to pick which trusts to bust; the Mann-Elkins Act, which brought the telephone and telegraph industries under control of the federal government; and the creation of the Department of Labor.

Split between Taft and Roosevelt
In the Congressional elections of 1910, the radical Progressives (known as the insurgents) were able, with the help of the Democrats, to diminish the power of the Old Guard republicans in the House. Meanwhile, President Taft drifted closer and closer to the side of the Old Guard. In 1909, Secretary of the Interior Richard Bollinger leased national land to corporations, incurring the wrath of forester Gifford Pinchot, who asked for a Senate investigation. Bollinger was forced to resign to take the heat off of Taft. In the Congressional election of 1910, former President Roosevelt announced a mixture of Progressive and Liberal ideas called the New Nationalism program and was labeled a

Marxist. Then, finally, Taft destroyed a merger between US Steel and Tennessee Coal and Iron that Roosevelt had supported, infuriating the former president.

Progressive Movement

The Progressive Movement was marked by advances in rights for workers, women and minorities. As the twentieth century began, it seemed as if the rich were getting richer and the poor were becoming more numerous. Per capita income and population had both increased dramatically, but wealth seemed to be concentrated in a smaller and smaller group. Between one-third and one-half of all factory workers lived in poverty and management showed no concern for these workers in the form of unemployment or worker's compensation. Many of the wealthy magnates felt the poor were that way because of their sinfulness and thus had no desire to provide aid. At the same time, many in the middle class feared that the lower class would revolt, although they didn't want to cause trouble themselves.

Summary of the Progressive Movement
It is important to note that Progressivism is not synonymous with Socialism; Progressives wanted to change the system, while Socialists wanted to destroy it altogether. Progressives believed that the government should regulate all business. Moreover, the Progressives wanted to take government out of the hands of the rich and put it into the hands of the common people. Often, Progressives had difficulty getting organized. This problem had been the death knell of the Populists; the Progressives were able to succeed in spite of their turmoil because they had great leaders: Roosevelt, Taft, and Wilson. The Progressive philosophy was started by a small minority of liberal intellectuals, including William James and Henry Adams. Among the authors who wrote on Progressive themes were Jacob Riis (How the Other Half Lives), Frank Norris (The Octopus, on railroad corruption), and Upton Sinclair (The Jungle, on corruption in the meatpacking industry).

Effects of Progressive Movement on women and farmers
During the early part of the twentieth century, women aggressively pursued more rights. Sarah Platt Decker led the General Federation of Women's Clubs, a group that worked hard to improve working conditions for women and children. The International Ladies' Garment Workers Union was also popular; it received a great deal of publicity after 146 women died in a fire at the Triangle Shirt factory. Jane Addams supported Prohibition, as did the Women's Christian Temperance Union and the Anti-Saloon League. Carrie A. Nation became famous for attacking saloons with an axe. For their part, farmers were doing much better in the early years of the twentieth century than in years past; those who were still struggling joined with the Progressives.

Labor unions, immigrants, and blacks
By 1914 the American Federation of Labor had 2 million members, although most Americans still did not trust labor unions. Meanwhile, immigrants had withstood several challenges to their legitimacy. The Immigration Restriction League had tried many times to require immigrants to pass a literacy test. For their part, immigrants were annoyed that they had to go to school, they hated Prohibition, and they hated the settlement houses into which they were often forced by the government. Blacks were one group that would not receive much help during the Progressive era. In 1905 W.E.B. DuBois had spearheaded the Niagara Movement, which led to the formation of the National Association for the

Advancement of Colored People. In 1911 the National Urban League was formed to help blacks move into the cities.

National reforms of the Progressive Movement

The 16th amendment (1913) allowed for an income tax. The 17th amendment (1913) provided for the direct election of US senators. The 18th amendment (1919) prohibited alcohol. The 19th amendment (1920) gave women the right to vote. In the case of Muller v. Oregon (1908), the Supreme Court upheld Oregon's 10-hour workday for women. In Hammer v. Dagerheart (1918), the Supreme Court declared the Keating-Owen Act of 1916 was unconstitutional. This act had prohibited interstate shipping of goods made in factories that employed children. The Court declared that the regulation of factories was the concern of the states. In response to this decision, many states passed acts banning child labor. The first minimum wage (25c) was established in Massachusetts in 1912. New York established the first lasting workman's compensation rules in 1910. In 1896, Utah had become the first state to limit the workday, to ten hours.

Social critics and state reforms during the Progress Movement

Eugene V. Debs was a prominent Socialist leader during the Progressive era. The Industrial Workers of the World, established in 1905 by "Big Bill" Haywood and known as the "Wobblies," was a radical and militant labor union that appealed to unskilled workers. There were some interesting state and local experiments in this period. In Galveston, Texas, the city switched to a commission system in which the heads of various departments were elected. In Staunton, Virginia, the office of the mayor was done away with in favor of a managing council. Robert LaFollette's many reforms in Wisconsin led Roosevelt to refer to this state as the "laboratory of democracy." LaFollette tied the university system, the railroads, and the banks to the state government. Governor Woodrow Wilson of New Jersey planned to use corporate taxes to pay for public education.

Establishment as a World Power

1920s

Election of 1920

The election of 1920 was known as the "solemn referendum." In it, Republican Warren G. Harding (who had voted against the League of Nations) defeated Democrat James Cox (who had Franklin Roosevelt as his running mate). Harding's election was in part due to his opposition to the League, but also it was due to his being a radical departure from Wilson. As the 1920s began, Americans felt disillusioned: few people felt that WWI would be the end of war, and massive immigration had left the US scrambling for an identity. There was also hostility lingering from the war: anti-radical, anti-immigration, anti-black, and anti-urban groups had broad followings. The general negativity at the beginning of the decade was not helped by the post-war recession and a massive outbreak of influenza that killed half a million people.

Harding presidency

When Warren G. Harding came into office he promised a "return to normalcy." He almost immediately passed the Esch-Cummins Act of 1920 which allowed for virtual trusts in the railroad industry. Harding raised tariffs and was known for having a strong Cabinet, which included Herbert Hoover as Secretary of Commerce. Harding's administration was also known for a large number of scandals. It was discovered at one point that Attorney General Harry Daugherty was selling pardons, parole, and liquor; his successor, Jesse Smith, was later found to be doing exactly the same thing. In the Forbes Scandal, the head of the Veterans Bureau was found to have embezzled $250 million from the organization. In the Teapot Dome Scandal, the Secretary of the Interior was discovered to have sold government oil reserves to private interests. Near the end of his term, Harding had a stroke and was succeeded by Calvin Coolidge.

Race relations in the early 1920s

In July 1919, there were violent race riots because of competition for jobs; in Chicago, a black swimmer crossed into the wrong area of Lake Michigan, sparking another riot. At around this time, the KKK increased in popularity in part because of D.W. Griffith's movie "Birth of a Nation," which depicted the Old South as a paradise led by the Klan. The KKK was led by Hiram Evans and had between 4 and 5 million members; it was anti-black, anti-immigration, anti-Jewish, anti-Catholic, and anti-alcohol. Membership in the Klan declined slightly in the wake of some lynchings and as the economy improved. Nevertheless, many blacks sought refuge in the big cities, as part of the Great Black Migration. Also at this time, the Harlem Renaissance was reinvigorating black culture: this movement included Langston Hughes, Countee Cullen, Duke Ellington, Paul Robeson, and Louis Armstrong. Many blacks subscribed to the beliefs of Marcus Garvey, who thought blacks should return to Africa.

Immigration and labor issues

The radical International Workers of the World was defunct by 1920, but many people still feared the influx of new ideas (including communism) and immigrants to the US. Indeed, immigrants became the scapegoat for many of the nation's problems. With the Immigration Restriction Act of 1921, only a certain quota of immigrants would be allowed into the country. The National Origins Act of 1924 restricted immigration even further, and stipulated that no Japanese would be allowed into the US. Basically, Americans only wanted Nordics to be able to enter the country. Anti-communist sentiment flared up for the first time during this period; A. Mitchell Palmer, the attorney general under Wilson, encouraged citizens to "rouse the Reds."

Provincialism vs. Modernity in the 1920s
At the beginning of the 1920s, the American population was evenly divided between city-dwellers and country-dwellers. While the cities were booming in the post-war period, farmers found themselves in economic trouble because of their surpluses. At around this time many writers including Ernest Hemingway, F. Scott Fitzgerald and the members of the Ashcan School sharply criticized the growing materialism of the urbanites. In 1920, the "noble experiment" of Prohibition began; it was constantly undermined by corrupt government and organized crime, and the government lost the money it had made on the taxation of alcohol. Another incident which brought the differences between Americans into sharp relief was the Scopes Monkey Trial in Dayton, Tennessee (1925). In this trial, Clarence Darrow successfully defended a science teacher who had taught the students Darwin's theory of natural selection.

US response to the Treaty of Versailles and the League of Nations

The US Senate rejected both the Treaty of Versailles and the League of Nations. Republicans, including Henry Cabot Lodge, created the "Round Robin Manifesto" guaranteeing that the Treaty would not be approved; some felt that the Republicans were hurt that none of their members had been invited to the table in Versailles. Other politicians were simply angry that the Kaiser had not been killed. Wilson attempted to take the matter of the treaty directly to the American people but he suffered a stroke in 1919 and both the Treaty and the League were rejected by Congress. Lodge issued the Lodge Reservations, a rebuttal to Wilson's Fourteen Points, in which he declared that it was an infringement on Congress' power for Wilson to assert that the US military would be used to protect other nations. In the national climate of isolationism and disillusionment that followed the war, it was perhaps inevitable that the US would never sign the Treaty or join the League.

Coolidge presidency and the election of 1924

Calvin Coolidge succeeded Harding after the latter succumbed to a stroke; Coolidge then won the election of 1924 by distancing himself from the scandals of the Coolidge administration. He is famous for saying, "The business of America is business," and his administration embodied that credo. He allowed the return of trusts (now known as "mergers") and he made major efforts to protect American business abroad. When struggling farmers looked to the government for help, Coolidge responded by vetoing the McNary-Haugan Bill, which would have established a minimum price for agricultural products. The Clayton Anti-trust Act was totally ignored during the Coolidge presidency.

Election of 1928 and Hoover's agricultural program

The election of 1928 pitted Herbert Hoover of the Republicans against Alfred E. Smith of the Democrats. Hoover, who had served as Secretary of Commerce under Harding, was associated with rural voters, Prohibition, and Protestantism and earned a solid victory over Smith after a dirty campaign. Hoover immediately put into action his "self-help" program for agriculture. With the Agricultural Marketing Act he established cooperatives. He also established the Federal Farm Board to loan money to farmers and the Grain and Cotton Stabilization Corporation to buy surpluses. Hoover passed the Hawley-Smoot Tariff of 1930, which allowed the president to adjust the tariff at his own discretion; Hoover set it at the highest peacetime rate in American history.

Hoover and the Great Depression

Hoover's first strategy for combating the Great Depression was to balance the budget, reduce federal spending, keep the US on the gold standard, and just wait it out. Later, he developed some work-relief programs, employing people on public work projects. The Hoover Dam was one of those projects. Hoover also created the Reconstruction Finance Group, which loaned money directly to state and local governments as well as to railroads and banks. Hoover's aid projects were unprecedented; still, he resisted giving direct aid to the people in the form of welfare. World War I veterans descended on Washington in 1932 when they were told that their pensions would not be paid until 1945. These so-called "Bonus Marchers" eventually had to be dispersed with force, leading many citizens to believe that the country was descending into anarchy. The 20th amendment, known as the anti-Hoover amendment, actually brought the date of the next inauguration forward.

Causes of the Great Depression
The Great Depression was the result of a number of converging factors. For one thing, there was an agricultural depression in the 1920s brought on by tremendous post-war surpluses. The automobile and housing industries both experienced diminished demand in the 20s. One major problem was that wealth was so unevenly distributed: one-third of the nation's wealth was controlled by 5% of the population. There was not much in the way of international trade, in part because of Hoover's high tariff. Overproduction on assembly lines led to factory surpluses and unemployment. Finally, there was persistent unsound speculation in the stock markets. By 1929, many stocks were considered to be overvalued and thus no one was buying them. This caused the catastrophic market crashes of Black Thursday and Black Tuesday (October 24 and 29, 1929), in which 40% of the market value (about $30 billion) was lost.

Franklin Delano Roosevelt

Franklin D. Roosevelt was elected president in the election of 1932. He was determined to preserve the US government and tried to calm the general public with his folksy "Fireside Chats." As the governor of New York, Roosevelt had been able to experiment with social welfare programs. He was a pragmatist and a follower of the Keynesian school of economics which insisted that the government had to spend money in order to get out of the Depression. Unlike Hoover, then, Roosevelt supported massive government spending and little volunteerism; he wanted the government to regulate agriculture and industry and also for it to take an interest in the daily economic decisions of the people.

In the early days of his term, FDR promoted the 3 Rs: relief, recovery, and reform. He announced a bank holiday for five days to stop the drain on the cash flow. The Emergency Banking Act authorized the Reconstruction Finance Group to buy bank stocks in order to finance repair. The Glass-Steagall Act made it illegal for banks to loan money to people for the purpose of playing the market and established the Federal Deposit Insurance Corporation to protect banks. The Economy Act cut $400 million from veterans' payments and $100 million from government salaries. Roosevelt had the gold standard and prohibition repealed. The Federal Emergency Relief Administration was established to provide $3 billion in direct relief to people.

As part of his New Deal program to help the US recover from the Great Depression, FDR established the First Agricultural Adjustment Administration. This agency provided farmers with loans to help them with mortgage payments and paid them not to plant or sell agricultural products. The formation of the AAA was economically successful, but was one of the least popular measures in the New Deal; it would later be declared unconstitutional in Butler v. US (1936). The Federal Securities Act stated that the securities dealers must disclose the prices of stocks and bonds. The Wagner Act of 1935 made it illegal for employers to have blacklists of unionized workers. The Federal Housing Administration was established to provide lower interest rates for people willing to repair or purchase a house. The US Housing Authority was created to loan money to state and local governments for the construction of low-cost housing.

The Civil Works Administration, headed by Harry Hopkins, was established to give people work. The Civilian Conservation Corps was a civilian army that built things such as the Blue Ridge Parkway. Other organizations created to employ people were the Public Works Administration, the Works Progress Administration, the Tennessee Valley Authority (responsible for the construction of 21 dams), the National Youth Administration (gave work to high school students) and the Rural Electrification Administration. The National Industrial Recovery Act tried to encourage fair competition and create scarcity to drive prices up. It established a minimum wage, a maximum number of weekly hours, and the right of labor to organize. In Schechter Poultry v. US (1935), the Supreme Court would rule that the NIRA should have been made up of laws instead of codes, because there were too many loopholes.

Resistance to FDR's New Deal
Father Coughlin was a priest who became famous for his radio broadcasts; he blamed the banks and an "international Jewish conspiracy" for the Depression. Dr. Francis E. Townsend was a famous advocate for senior citizens who advocated a national sales tax. Alf Landon ran against FDR in the 1936 presidential election, and was defeated soundly because of his ties to big business. In the "Court Packing" controversy of 1937, FDR tried to overcome Supreme Court resistance to the New Deal by increasing the number of justices on the Court from 9 to 15. This attempt was unsuccessful, but Roosevelt was able to fill Court vacancies with New Deal supporters. A final bit of resistance to the New Deal occurred during the so-called "Roosevelt Recession" of 1937-8, in which the economy seemed to be making much less progress than before. Many historians attribute this recession to the fact that New Deal programs were getting much less use in this era.

Black Americans and the Great Depression

In the Scottsboro (AL) case of 1932, 9 young black men were accused of raping 2 white women. Although the evidence was scant, all 9 of the men were convicted. In Powell v. Alabama, the Supreme Court would rule that the men had not been given a fair trial because they had not had adequate representation. At around this time, the white Harold Ickes was the head of the NAACP. He worked hard to get New Deal jobs for blacks, Thurgood Marshall among them. Eleanor Roosevelt also was an advocate for blacks in this period. She came into open conflict with the Daughters of the American Revolution after this group denied

Marian Anderson, a black opera singer, the right to sing at Constitution Hall. In general, the New Deal helped many blacks obtain leadership positions that otherwise would have been closed to them. The Roosevelt administration was the first to show any real concern for blacks, so most blacks became life-long Democrats.

Woodrow Wilson

Woodrow Wilson appointed William Jennings Bryant as his Secretary of State; Bryant became known for his policy of "cooling off," wherein volatile situations would be ignored until all parties had a chance to reconsider their positions. One of Wilson's first major acts as president was to push through the Underwood-Simmons Tariff of 1913. This reduces the duty rate to 27% and drastically reduced the tariff on a thousand other items. It also included a slightly greater income tax. Another important economic move was the Federal Reserve Act of 1913: this set up a national banking system to be overseen by a Federal Reserve Board. The Federal Reserve system would become the first effective national banking system since the Second Bank of the United States, and would be one of the great legacies of Wilson's term. It gave the government a ready means to adjust the amount of currency in circulation.

Wilson's affect on trusts
When Wilson entered office, he declared that there was no such thing as a good trust. With the Federal Trade Commission Act of 1914, a bi-partisan committee of 5 was created to investigate trusts and issue reports to the government and to the public. The creation of the FTC slowed the growth of monopolies. Peeved by the ineffectiveness of the Sherman Anti-trust Act, Wilson supported the passage of the Clayton Anti-trust Act of 1914. This prohibited business from selling at reduced prices to favored customers if this price discrimination helped create a monopoly. It also prevented so-called "tying contracts," which forbade a purchaser from buying or selling the products of a competitor. The act also outlawed large interlocking directories; formally allowed the existence of labor unions and farm organizations, as well as strikes and boycotts; and declared that no injunctions could be issued unless property was at stake.

Wilson's Moral Diplomacy
Along with his Secretary of State William Jennings Bryant, Woodrow Wilson promoted the view that nations should treat one another ethically. For instance, the Panama Canal Tolls Act of 1912 had made it so that the US did not have to pay tolls to use the canal, unlike every other nation; Wilson did away with this measure. Wilson's actions in the Dominican Republic were more dubious. The Dominican Republic had been in deep debt early in the twentieth century, and the Roosevelt administration had been glad to help in exchange for keeping some troops in the country. When in 1916 the Dominican Republic asked the US to leave, Wilson refused and sent in the Marines. It was only in 1940 that the Dominican Republic was no longer considered a US protectorate. A similar scenario occurred in Haiti: the US offered to help the tiny nation, but was unwilling to leave when asked (mainly because of economic interest).

Wilson's New Freedom agenda
The Smith-Lever Act of 1914 brought public education into rural areas. The Smith-Hughes Act of 1917 allocated money for vocational training and home economics courses. The Federal Farm Loan Act of 1916 divided the US into 12 agricultural districts, and established federal farm loan banks with low interest rates. The Adamson Act of 1916 asserted that

- 59 -

railway workers should be paid for a 10-hour day, though they should only be required to work 8 hours. During Wilson's presidency, Lewis Brandeis became the first Jewish member of the Supreme Court. In general, then, Wilson believed in regulating business and improving social welfare. He did not, however, see anything wrong with segregation.

World War I

America's role in the build-up to World War I
There had been relative peace in Europe since the end of the Napoleonic Wars in 1815. Many even felt that the age of great wars was over. In 1910, the US had become involved in the Pan-American Union, which was organized to settle differences with diplomacy rather than violence. At the First Hague Conference in 1899, 26 nations agreed on the principles of mediation, the humane rules of war, and on the creation of a permanent court of arbitration. At the Second Hague Conference in 1907, 44 nations reaffirmed the old agreements and declared that the payment of debts could not be forced through war. Unfortunately, there would be no Third Hague Conference; it was cancelled due to World War I.

US attempts at neutrality
For a while, the US tried to remain impartial in World War I, not least because it was making a great deal of money producing supplies for both sides. Among the general public, there was general support for Britain and France, but many German and Irish immigrants supported the Central powers. There were a small group of American citizens who flew missions for the French, known as the Lafayette Escadrille. Gradually, the US government became angry with both sides, even as it tried to maintain trade with both sides. The British blockade of neutral Scandinavia annoyed the US, as did the German's flouting of the rules of war with their aggressive U-boats. In 1915, the British ship Lusitania was sunk off the coast of Ireland, killing 128 Americans. This convinced many Americans that neutrality could not be maintained.

Causes of World War I
The rise in nationalism at the beginning of the twentieth century helped contribute to the possibility of war. There was also some conflict between the imperialist (France, Britain, and the US) and the non-imperialist (Germany, Italy) nations. Many large nations were seeking economic expansion outside of their own borders, and the competition for foreign markets was intense. There was also a complex system of entangling alliances; many countries were involved in several different alliances at the same time. The spark for World War I, though, was the assassination of Archduke Franz Ferdinand, heir to the throne of Austria-Hungary, in April of 1914 by a Serbian nationalist. When Emperor Franz Joseph declared war on Serbia, it set off a chain reaction that involved virtually every nation in Europe.

US and the Mexican Revolution
Mexicans traditionally resented the US for its seizure of Texas and the Southwest. When the US-friendly leader Porfirio Diaz was overthrown in 1910, and eventually replaced by the murderous dictator Victorian Huerto, the US sent weapons to his opponents. Then, in April 1914, two American soldiers of the USS Tampico were jailed in Mexico and the US did not receive an apology upon their release. This angered the US, and they in turn seized a German ship that was believed to be unloading war materials to Mexico. The only thing that kept the US out of a more serious conflict was the ABC Mediation: Argentina, Brazil, and Chile met and convinced Huerto to retire. Still, Pancho Villa, a challenger for control of

Mexico, continued to antagonize the US; he killed several Americans and was unsuccessfully pursued by American forces.

Election of 1916 and entrance into WWI
In the election of 1916, Wilson narrowly defeated the Republican Charles Evans Hughes. Wilson ran on a peace platform. Soon after, however, diplomatic relations were broken off with the Central powers, and submarine warfare began. The American entrance to WWI was accelerated by the "Zimmermann Note," in which the German minister to Mexico encouraged that country to attack the United States. In 1917, merchant vessels were ordered by Wilson to arm themselves. Among the reasons the US sided with the Allies was the fact that American business was more deeply connected with these countries than with the Central powers. Also, the US had traditionally had stronger ties with Britain and France.

Increasing American involvement
During the early years of WWI, the tide of nationalism was rising in the US. Many people felt it would be impossible for America to remain neutral; even Theodore Roosevelt decried conscientious objectors. Nevertheless, many pacifists objected to any involvement. William Jennings Bryant resigned as Secretary of State after the sinking of the Lusitania, advising the US to stay off of British ships; to stop selling weapons to both sides; and to not side so unthinkingly with the British. At around this time, Roosevelt began recruiting and training men as part of the Plattsburg Experiment. Finally, Wilson increased the number of troops in both the Army and the Navy with the National Defense Act of 1916. Wilson also set into motion a campaign to build more ships.

Contributions of the American public to WWI and public opinion of the war
The 18th amendment to the Constitution, otherwise known as the Volstead Act, outlawed alcohol in 1920. This amendment was purported to conserve food, though it was really an attempt to influence public morality. Through the Food Administration, Wilson encouraged people to plant "victory gardens," and to skip meat one day a week. The war was also supported through the Espionage and Sedition Acts of 1917-8, which made it illegal to say negative things about the war or to interfere with the sale of war bonds. In Schenck v. US (1919), the arrest of the Socialist leader Charles Schenck for criticizing the war was upheld by the Supreme Court which asserted that First Amendment rights were only exercisable when they did not present a clear and present danger to the nation. In Abrams v. US (1919), a Russian immigrant critical of the US actions in Russian was also declared to be a clear and present danger.

Wilson's war agenda
On April 2, 1917, Wilson addressed the nation on the subject of World War I. He declared that the conduct of the German U-boats was "a war against humanity itself," and that, if managed successfully, WWI would be "a war to make the world safe for democracy." Four days later, a declaration of war was passed. The Selective Service Act of 1917 registered and drafted millions of American men for military service; about 4.7 million Americans served in the war. The American war effort was mainly paid for with borrowed money, though an increased income tax and the sale of war bonds contributed. Wilson also mobilized American industry; the War Industries Board, headed by Bernard Baruch, strove to cut waste and create new industries to aid the war effort. The National War Labor Board, headed by ex-President Taft, tried to streamline the labor force to aid the war effort.

Wilson's Fourteen Point program

Wilson issued his Fourteen Point program supposedly to try to create a quick and lasting peace. Also, however, Wilson hoped to draw the Russians back into the war, to inspire the war-weary Allies, and to demoralize the enemy nations by appealing to the dissenting contingents. Some of the changes called for in the Fourteen Points were open diplomacy, freedom of the seas, no tariffs, reduced land artilleries, right of self-determination for all people, a temporary international control of colonies (not imperialism) and the creation of the League of Nations. Wilson's proposal encouraged the Slavic peoples in Germany and Austria-Hungary to resist the war. Its success in defusing the German war effort allowed Wilson to insist that he would only negotiate with a ruler of the people's choice; Kaiser Wilhelm was forced to abdicate the throne.

Perception of American soldiers

The situation for the Allies was desperate after Russia left the war under the Brest-Litovsk Treaty of 1917. The US began to convoy British and French ships in an attempt to prevent U-boat attacks. The American soldiers in Europe were referred to as Doughboys, Yanks, and Devil Dogs. Some of the American heroes in the war were Alvin York ("Sergeant York"), who reportedly killed 20 and captured 132; J.J. Pershing, who led the American Expeditionary Force; and Eddie Rickenbacker, a pilot credited with 22 kills. Americans were praised for their efforts at Cantigny, Reims, and in the Argonne Forest campaign, where there were over 128,000 American casualties.

US and the League of Nations

The League of Nations had five permanent members: Japan, Britain, Italy, France, and the US. Germany and Russia were not included. The League would have a General Assembly and a Court of International Justice. It would try to use economic sanctions and, if necessary, force to guarantee the territorial integrity and political independence of every nation. The problems the League developed in practice were many: it was almost impossible to set into motion, because a unanimous vote was required for action; it created a number of artificial and unsuccessful countries (Sudetenland, for example); it had no power to regulate economics; it excluded two major nations (Russia and Germany); and it had no power to force a nation to disarm.

Armistice of WWI and the Treaty of Versailles

On November 11, 1918, the Germans agreed to an armistice provided that Wilson's Fourteen Points be used as a treaty. Overall, between 9 and 10 million people died in the war, including 320,000 Americans. In the Treaty of Versailles (1919), the League of Nations was created to handle international disputes. A number of new countries such as Poland and Czechoslovakia, were created by this treaty; also, Germany was disarmed and forced to pay war reparations. Later, the Treaty of Versailles would come to be seen as an uneasy mixture of vengeance and conciliation. It also relied too much on the good faith of the signers. Wilson recognized many problems with the treaty, but he felt the League of Nations would be able to correct them in the future.

World War II

Latin American foreign policy from 1920 to 1945

The US had tremendous financial investments in Latin America and most of the government's policy there was aimed at securing these investments. In 1921, the US paid $21 million to Colombia, in part for stealing the land for the Panama Canal and in part to

- 62 -

keep them from seizing US oil investments. At this time, the US also had bad relations with Mexico until the election there of President Calles, a pro-American politician. During the Hoover administration, the US tried to promote "good neighborism" with respect to Mexico and the rest of Latin America. In 1934, the Platt Amendment gave Cuba full independence. When Batista came to power, however, the US backed him completely and refused to acknowledge any other elected leaders.

America's introduction to WWII

After the First World War, the US became obsessed with isolating itself from foreign conflicts. The Nye Committee studied the war, and determined that it had been fought for financial reasons, and could have been avoided. Isolationist parties achieved some popularity during this period, including the America First Committee, led by Charles Lindbergh, and SOS (Stop Organized Slaughter). The Neutrality Laws of 1935-7 declared that the US could not sell weapons to another country in a time of war, and that US citizens could not travel on the ships of a nation at war. In 1937, FDR delivered the Quarantine Speech, in which he asserted that the Nazi "disease" must be contained. Finally, after conflict in Europe had escalated considerably, FDR declared that the US needed to help Britain, and be an "arsenal of democracy in the world." The Neutrality Act of 1940 made it legal for the US to sell weapons on a cash and carry basis. In August of 1941, FDR and Churchill drew up the Atlantic Charter, which vowed to destroy Nazism, protect the right of self-determination, and create a Word Peace Organization.

Buildup to the attack on Pearl Harbor

A number of events had created a stormy relationship between the US and Japan long before the invasion of Pearl Harbor. The US influence over the Treaty of Portsmouth, which ended the Russo-Japanese War, created a great deal of tension between the two countries. The Japanese were also antagonized by Theodore Roosevelt's parade of the Great White Fleet, and by the National Origins Act of 1924 and the Segregation Laws, which kept Japanese from entering and assimilating into the US. America also had a cordial relationship at this time with Japan's longtime rival, China. As the Japanese became more belligerent, the US froze all Japanese assets in America and denied Japan the purchase of any more oil or scrap metal. The Japanese then launched surprise attacks both on the American naval base at Pearl Harbor and on the Philippines, where they hoped to secure some oil.

Election of 1940 and the American home front during WWII

In 1940, FDR easily defeated the Republican Wendell Wilkie. After his election, Roosevelt pledged that every resource would be devoted to winning the war. FDR created a number of war-time bureaucracies including the War Production Board (which was devoted to manufacturing goods for war), the War Manpower Commission (which organized the draft and created jobs for women) and the Office of Price Administration, which set prices and rations. In total, the US war effort cost between $330 and $360 billion. Most of this cost was covered through taxation and the sale of government bonds. The US frequently denied civil liberties to Japanese-Americans during this period, forcing many to live in internment camps. In Korematsu v. US (1944), the Supreme Court ruled that the internment camps were legal, but in ex parte Endo (1944), the Court adjusted its decision to state that the US could only intern those whose disloyalty could be proven.

US involvement in WWII concerning Europe and Africa

After the Japanese attack on Pearl Harbor in 1941, the US declared war on Japan, after which Germany declared war on the US. Before going after Japan, however, the US first attacked Germany; this was done because the US underestimated Japan industrially and militarily, and because the US feared Britain was on the verge of defeat. Operation Overlord, the Allied invasion of the European continent at Normandy, was led in part by General Dwight D. Eisenhower. The American generals Omar Bradley and George Patton took part in the Allied Operation Torch, aimed at taking back North Africa. At the Battle of the Bulge, in Belgium, the Germans tried to break the Allied lines, but were unsuccessful, in part because of the heroism of American soldiers.

US involvement in WWII concerning Asia and the Pacific

The US strategy for controlling the Pacific was known as "island hopping." In the Coral Sea Battle of 1942, Americans stopped the Japanese from taking Australia and New Guinea. In the same year, the Doolittle raids of Japanese naval bases boosted American morale. In the Battle of Midway (1942), the US sunk four Japanese aircraft carriers. In the Battle of Leyte Gulf, General Douglas MacArthur took back the Philippines, and also took control of Iwo Jima and Okinawa. During this period, a team of American scientists led by Robert Oppenheimer were developing the atomic bomb in Los Alamos, New Mexico. Japan was warned several times by President Truman that the bomb would be used if they did not surrender. Surely enough, Americans dropped atomic bombs on Hiroshima on August 6, 1945, and on Nagasaki three days later. Japanese leaders surrendered aboard the USS Missouri on August 15, 1945.

Yalta Conference

The Yalta Conference was held on an island in the Crimean Sea in February of 1945. It was attended by FDR, Churchill, and Stalin. At the Conference, FDR tried to make sure that Germany would not be split into smaller nations (this would happen later). Stalin "liberated" the countries along the border of Nazi Germany, and in exchange FDR allowed the Red Army to remain in those countries. This Conference established boundaries and a provisional government for Poland (this provisional government was led by the Soviets, and would last until 1989). One of the more important moves of this Conference was that the US and Britain allowed a Communist government under Mao Zedong to remain in Mongolia; this group of Communists would eventually take over China in 1949.

Truman and the Fair Deal

When Truman came into office after the death of Franklin Roosevelt in 1945, he was already fighting an uphill battle. Many people felt that the Democrats had controlled the executive branch for too long, and many expected Truman to have the personal charisma of FDR. Truman gamely attempted to continue the reforms of the New Deal, which he renamed the Fair Deal. Nevertheless, he was frequently thwarted by the Republican Congress. Truman surprisingly won a narrow victory over Dewey in the election of 1948, and continued to pursue reforms in education, health care, and civil rights. He gradually became worn down by his conflicts with Congress, however, and he declined to run in 1952.

Modern Era

Korean War

The Korean War took place during the Truman presidency. Korea had been divided after WWII into a northern half (under Soviet control) and a southern half (under American control). When foreign troops finally withdrew from the peninsula, North Korea attacked South Korea in an attempt to unify. The United Nations Security Council declared that North Korea was an aggressor, and sent troops led by the American General Douglas MacArthur to the region. MacArthur had some early victories, but progress slowed when China began to send men and supplies to the North Koreans. Gradually, combat gave way to armistice talks, yet those these too seemed to drag on endlessly.

Dwight Eisenhower

Election of 1952 and Eisenhower
General Dwight Eisenhower, a Republican, defeated the Democrat Adlai Stevenson in the election of 1952. One of the first crises of the Eisenhower administration concerned the Suez Canal in Egypt. The conflict began after Israel attacked Egypt in response to attacks on the new Jewish nation that were launched at Egyptian bases; at the same time, England and France withdrew plans to build a dam on the Suez Canal because of Egypt's recognition of Communist China. Angered by these events, the Egyptian President Nasser seized the assets of the European company that administered traffic on the canal. The United States was eventually able to defuse the situation; this marked the introduction of the so-called Eisenhower Doctrine, in which American troops and money would be used to undermine Communism in various regions around the world.

Civil rights under Eisenhower
For a long time, the problems of blacks had been considered a Southern issue; however, massive black migration into the Northern cities made civil rights a national question. In Brown v. Board of Education (1954), the Supreme Court ruled that segregation in public schools is unconstitutional. After some southern states defied this decision, Eisenhower was forced to send in federal troops. At the same time, blacks were staging nonviolent protests across the south. Rosa Parks famously refused to give up her bus seat in Montgomery, Alabama, and four black men staged a sit-in at a whites-only lunch counter in Greensboro, North Carolina. With the Civil Rights Acts of 1957 and 1960, blacks were given the right to vote; these acts were not enforced.

US foreign policy under Eisenhower
The Secretary of State under Eisenhower was John Foster Dulles, who wanted to pursue an aggressive foreign policy to "roll back Communism." This was also the period in which the national defense budget skyrocketed, as both the US and USSR believed that peace could be maintained by threatening the other side with total annihilation. It was in this climate that the US first became involved in Vietnam. The French had been kicked out of this Southeast Asian nation for good in 1954, and the country had been divided into a northern and southern half in the Geneva Truce of the same year. The US then tried to bolster the standing of the non-communist leader Ngo Dinh Diem in the south, as he batted the communist Viet Cong. Increasingly, Eisenhower was funneling money to the anti-

communist forces in South Vietnam, believing that if this country became communist, others would follow (the "Domino effect").

Anti-communism in the United States

As the US was becoming more embroiled in the Cold War, Americans became increasingly paranoid about the spread of Communism. There were numerous investigations aimed at weeding Communist spies out of the government, and two people, Julius and Ethel Rosenberg, were executed for spying. The leader of much of this was Senator Joseph McCarthy, who was famous for promoting and prolonging the "Red Scare" as the often-termed witch-hunt for communists in the government was known (Soviet communications released after the fall of the Soviet Union confirmed the vast majority of his accusations). The tide of anti-communism extended into a general disapproval of organized labor. The Taft-Hartley Act restricted the ability of labor unions markedly. In order to survive, the nation's two largest labor unions combined, forming the AFL-CIO.

John F. Kennedy

In the election of 1960, the Democrat John F. Kennedy defeated Richard Nixon; this was the first election in which television was a major factor. One of the most important issues of the Kennedy presidency would be the space race with the Soviet Union. It was under Kennedy that the National Aeronautics and Space Administration was established. Alan Shepard became the first American in space in 1961, and in 1969 Neil Armstrong would become the first human to walk on the moon. Kennedy, unfortunately, would not witness this event: he was shot and killed by Lee Harvey Oswald in Dallas in November of 1963. Though some still claim that Oswald was a part of a broader conspiracy, an investigation led by Chief Justice Earl Warren declared that he had acted alone.

Civil rights during the Kennedy years
The black struggle for civil rights intensified during the Kennedy administration. After integration at Southern universities was mandated, National Guardsmen were deployed to keep the peace. The situation was especially tense in Alabama, where Governor George Wallace declared that segregation would stand in his state forever. In July of 1963, Martin Luther King led the famous March on Washington, during which he made his "I Have a Dream" speech. King would receive the Nobel Peace Prize in 1964. The 23rd and 24th amendments to the Constitution were aimed at redressing the issue of black suffrage; they gave electoral votes to Washington, DC, and eliminated the poll tax.

Lyndon Baines Johnson

Lyndon Baines Johnson took over as president after the assassination of Kennedy. He was able to use the "ghost" of the assassinated president to pass the Civil Rights Act of 1964. Johnson also declared a "war on poverty," a system of programs aimed at helping the poor. In the election of 1964, the escalating conflict in Vietnam was much in the public's mind, and the Republican candidate, Barry Goldwater, was viewed as a war-monger. The election of Johnson, however, did not keep the US out of Vietnam. After being elected, Johnson promoted legislation under the banner of the "Great Society." He created Medicare and Medicaid with the Social Security Act of 1965 and established the agency of Housing and Urban Development.

Foreign policy under Johnson

After an American ship came under fire from North Vietnam in the Gulf of Tonkin, Johnson received a blank check for American involvement in the region. General Westmoreland oversaw troops during this period of escalation. Soon, 184,000 American soldiers were in Vietnam, and the government was spending a million dollars every day. Coupled with inflation, this expense bled Johnson's domestic program dry. The peace movement in the US took off during this period. Many people protested what they saw as inequities in the draft system (for instance, blacks seemed to be unfairly overrepresented). The US problems in Vietnam were exposed to the world during the Tet Offensive of January 1968; during this period, the Viet Cong damaged American forces in virtually every city in the region.

Civil rights movement during the Johnson years

The summer of 1964 saw more violence in the South as three civil rights workers were murdered while trying to register voters. After the passage of the Voting Rights Act of 1965, Johnson would have to deploy Federal Marshals to escort blacks to the polls. Frustrated by the slow advance to equality, many blacks became more militant. During the summer of 1967, there were riots in 150 cities, most of which were sparked by economic concerns, as blacks felt they were being mistreated in the marketplace. Advocates of Black Power joined groups like the Black Panthers and the Mau Mau, and even formerly moderate groups like the SNCC would begin to endorse violence. Many white Americans who sympathized with the black struggle were alienated by this militancy. There were more riots in 1968 after the assassination of Martin Luther King in Memphis. The Civil Rights Act of 1968 gave full rights to blacks, but contained restrictions aimed at reducing racial violence.

Richard M. Nixon

Domestic policy of Nixon

In the election of 1968, the Republican Richard M. Nixon, who had narrowly lost to Kennedy in 1960, defeated the Democrat Hubert Humphrey. The Democratic National Convention had endured violent protests over the Vietnam War. Though much of Nixon's administration would be concerned with the war (and later with the Watergate investigation), he did institute a somewhat successful policy of sharing revenue with states. The economy was languishing in a state of stagflation (high inflation and high unemployment) during this period and thus Nixon tried to jolt it with a ninety-day wage and price freeze. This move, known as the New Economic Policy (or Nixonomics) was a total failure.

Vietnam

Nixon had won the election on a platform of "Peace with Honor," and upon entering office he began slowly withdrawing troops from Vietnam. The Nixon Doctrine asserted that the US would honor its commitment to South Vietnam with material rather than men. Nixon did, however, order an invasion of purportedly neutral Cambodia, where the Viet Cong were stockpiling weapons. It was also during Nixon's presidency that four students at Kent State University were killed by the National Guard during a protest. In the election of 1972, Nixon crushed George McGovern after Foreign Advisor Henry Kissinger claimed that peace was "at hand." After the election, Kissinger and Le Duc Tho would negotiate the Paris Peace Accords of 1973.

Domestic policy of Nixon
In the election of 1968, the Republican Richard M. Nixon, who had narrowly lost to Kennedy in 1960, defeated the Democrat Hubert Humphrey. The Democratic National Convention had endured violent protests over the Vietnam War. Though much of Nixon's administration would be concerned with the war (and later with the Watergate investigation), he did institute a somewhat successful policy of sharing revenue with states. The economy was languishing in a state of stagflation (high inflation and high unemployment) during this period and thus Nixon tried to jolt it with a ninety-day wage and price freeze. This move, known as the New Economic Policy (or Nixonomics) was a total failure.

Watergate scandal
On June 17, 1972, a break-in was thwarted at the Democratic National Committee office at the Watergate Hotel in Washington, DC. It was eventually discovered that the burglars had ties to the Nixon administration. This began the unraveling of an enormous conspiracy of corruption in the Nixon administration. Many of Nixon's advisers would be forced to resign, though Nixon still refused to cooperate with the investigation. Eventually, though, evidence would mount against him, and Nixon would be forced to release tapes of his Oval Office conversations. Nixon resigned on August 8, 1974, although he never admitted any guilt. The Watergate scandal left a permanent stain on the presidency.

Gerald Ford

Gerald Ford, a congressman from Michigan, had been appointed vice president under Nixon after the resignation of Spiro Agnew, and after the resignation of Nixon he became president. His was a mostly uneventful term, as the nation recovered from the shocks of Vietnam and Watergate. Ford talked a great deal about battling inflation, but never did very much to back up his rhetoric. It was during the Ford administration that South Vietnam fell once and for all to the North Vietnamese. Ford's most famous act may have been his full pardon of Nixon. Though Ford at the time declared that "our long national nightmare is over," this unpopular move may have cost him the election in 1976.

Jimmy Carter

Election of 1976 and the Carter administration
The Democratic governor of Georgia, Jimmy Carter, defeated the incumbent Gerald Ford in the election of 1976. Carter was popular with black voters, and was generally believed to be outside the cesspool of Washington politics. Carter immediately made an $18 billion tax cut, and inflation soared. Carter also made the controversial move of pardoning all those who evaded the draft during the Vietnam War. As for foreign policy, Carter became known for his humanitarian efforts: working for peace between Israel and Egypt at Camp David earned him the Nobel Peace Prize. Carter signed a bill to give the Panama Canal back to the Panamanians, and endured a severe oil shortage. This, along with the failed rescue of fifty American hostages in Iran, led to Carter's defeat in 1980.

Ronald Reagan

Election of 1980 and foreign policy under Reagan
In the election of 1980, known as the Conservative Revolution, Ronald Reagan easily defeated Jimmy Carter. Reagan presided over the last few years of the Cold War. In 1983,

Reagan authorized the invasion of Grenada, where there was an airstrip that was supposedly being used by the Cubans and the Soviet Union. Later in 1983, a Marine barrack in Lebanon was blown up by terrorists, killing hundreds of American soldiers. Reagan introduced the "Star Wars" program, a strategic defense initiative in which incoming missiles would be destroyed from outer space by laser-armed satellites. Reagan promoted the "Peace through strength" method of foreign policy, whereby the economic might of the United States would furnish such an intimidating military that the Soviet Union would be unable to compete financially and thus fail. This eventually played a major role in the fall of the Soviet Union in 1989. Reagan nevertheless improved relations with the Soviet Union diplomatically, even signing a treaty with Soviet Premier Mikhail Gorbachev to ban a certain class of Nuclear Weapon.

Domestic affairs under Reagan

Upon entering office, Reagan implemented tax cuts in the hopes of stimulating the economy. While this had a very positive effect on the economy by the end of his first term, the American trade deficit continued to grow wider. Reagan's presidency was tarnished by the Iran-Contra affair, in which it was determined that the US had sold weapons to a hostile nation. In 1984, due to an impressive economic recovery and unprecedented growth, Reagan defeated Walter Mondale (whose running mate was Geraldine Ferraro, the first female vice-presidential candidate) in a landslide, winning 49 states electorally. In the case Wallace v. Jaffree (1985), the Supreme Court ruled that schools could provide for a moment of silence, but could not endorse any particular religion. In US v. Eichman (1990), the Court ruled that burning the American flag qualified as expressive conduct, and was therefore permitted under the First Amendment.

George H.W. Bush

George Bush's foreign and domestic policies
In the election of 1988, the Republican Vice President George H.W. Bush defeated Michael Dukakis easily. Under Bush, the federal deficit continued to rise, and the US role in the Iran-Contra affair continued to cast a shadow over the executive branch. One of the major crises during the Bush administration was the wreck of the Exxon Valdez, which created the largest oil spill ever along the Alaskan coast. Meanwhile, Bush led the US military into the Persian Gulf War in 1990-1 after Iraq invaded neighboring Kuwait. American troops routed the Iraqis. It was also during Bush's administration that the Berlin Wall fell and the Communist regime in the Soviet Union finally crumbled.

Bill Clinton

Election of 1992 and domestic policy under Clinton
The Democratic governor of Arkansas, Bill Clinton, defeated the incumbent George H. W. Bush and H. Ross Perot (Independent) in the election of 1992. Clinton tried to reduce the federal deficit. He also pushed for gays to be allowed into the military. Clinton appointed Janet Reno as the first female Attorney General and also reversed most of the restrictions on abortions that had been established by the Reagan and Bush administrations. Clinton's presidency would be plagued by scandals throughout; he and his wife were accused of making illegal land deals in the Whitewater scandal and Clinton would later be impeached for lying under oath and obstructing justice in regard to an extramarital affair. A Democrat majority in the Senate elected not to remove him from office.

Election of 1996 and foreign policy under Clinton

In the election of 1996, the incumbent Bill Clinton narrowly defeated Kansas Senator Bob Dole. During Clinton's two terms, the United States trade deficit would continue. In the aftermath of the collapse of the Soviet regime, the US gave substantial aid to Russia and many of the new republics. The United States would also supply troops for a NATO peacekeeping effort during the Civil War in the former Yugoslavia between the years 1992 and 2000. American troops also participated in peacekeeping missions in Somalia, Bosnia, and Haiti. Finally, Clinton ordered air strikes against Iraq after it was determined that Iraqi leader Saddam Hussein had been part of a conspiracy to assassinate President Bush.

George W. Bush

Election of 2000

In the election of 2000, George W. Bush, the son of ex-President Bush, defeated Vice-President Al Gore, despite losing to Gore in the popular vote. Bush immediately instituted a major tax cut; critics claimed that this tax cut only benefited the very rich. On September 11, 2001, the US suffered the worst terrorist attack in its history, as four planes were hijacked and two of them destroyed the World Trade Center towers in New York. The attacks were planned and funded by al-Qaeda, an Islamic fundamentalist group led by Osama bin Laden. The United States almost immediately launched Operation Enduring Freedom, an attack on the Taliban government of Afghanistan that had harbored bin Laden.

Practice Test #1

Practice Questions

Use the excerpt and your knowledge of social studies to answer the following questions from the opening of the Declaration of Independence:

"IN CONGRESS, July 4, 1776.

The unanimous Declaration of the thirteen united States of America,

When in the Course of human events, it becomes necessary for one people to dissolve the political bands which have connected them with another, and to assume among the powers of the earth, the separate and equal station to which the Laws of Nature and of Nature's God entitle them, a decent respect to the opinions of mankind requires that they should declare the causes which impel them to the separation."

1. Which of the following sentences BEST summarizes the meaning of the excerpt?

Ⓐ The thirteen colonies were planning to give separate but equal rights to African-American slaves.

Ⓑ The thirteen colonies had been attacked by British troops, and wanted to list their reasons for fighting back against England.

Ⓒ The thirteen colonies were forming their own government separate from the King of England, and they planned to outline the reasons for their revolution against England.

Ⓓ The thirteen colonies would form their own government separate from England, but they would list the laws of nature which kept them attached to England for some purposes.

2. What grassroots political movement, started by southern and western farmers, arose in the 1890s U.S. to fight banks, railroads, large corporations and other "elites"?

Ⓐ Entrepreneurship Movement

Ⓑ Farmers United

Ⓒ Populist Movement

Ⓓ Social Gospel Movement

3. Which characteristic has NOT yet been used to define a historical era in U.S. History?

Ⓐ A land form

Ⓑ Years of war

Ⓒ Years of social reforms

Ⓓ A time of economic growth or failure

4. Which turning point event in the Spanish-American War occurred in 1898?

Ⓐ America gave financial support to Cuban nationalists' revolution against Spain.

Ⓑ Americans blamed Spain for the sinking of the *USS Maine*.

Ⓒ The Philippines declared independence from U.S. rule after Spain had transferred their rule of the Philippines to the U.S.

Ⓓ The U.S. withdrew from Cuba.

5. The 1887 General Allotment Act, also known as the Dawes Act, had a policy of giving private property ownership to Native Americans in order to divide the Native American reservations into individual "family farms." What was a practical result of this policy?

Ⓐ Many Native American tribes lost large portions of their reservations.

Ⓑ Many Native Americans became assimilated to the American culture of family farming.

Ⓒ The Nez Perce Conflict occurred between Nez Perce Native Americans and U.S. army forces.

Ⓓ American settlers moved to lands formerly owned by Native Americans and slaughtered most of the buffalo that Native Americans depended on for their livelihood.

6. In 1880, every state and territory in the U.S. had railway tracks. Which statement BEST describes an effect of railroad growth on the U.S. economy in the 1880s?

Ⓐ Railroad companies had to pay higher wages to employees

Ⓑ It provided better links between raw materials and markets

Ⓒ It increased competition between states and territories

Ⓓ It decreased taxes that railroad companies had to pay

Use the excerpt and your knowledge of social studies to answer the following question:
U.S. Navy Captain Alfred Thayer Mahan wrote an essay in 1890 including this statement:
"The interesting and significant feature of this changing attitude [in America] is the turning of the eyes outward, instead of inward only, to seek the welfare of the country."

7. In the above quote, what was Mahan correctly predicting would occur more often in the 1890s?

Ⓐ U.S. expansionism

Ⓑ U.S. western settlement

Ⓒ U.S. entry into World War I

Ⓓ U.S. census bureau increasing counts

Use the timeline and your knowledge of social studies to answer the following question:
Timeline of Events in Puerto Rico's History

1902   United States declares Puerto Rico a territory

1904   Unionist Party of Puerto Rico forms as political opposition against the colonial U.S. government

1914   Native Puerto Rican islanders' form a majority in the government's Executive Cabinet for this first time in the island's history as a U.S. territory

1917   President Wilson signs the Jones Act which made Puerto Rico an "organized but unincorporated" territory, gave the island more autonomy in their government, and gave U.S. citizen status to Puerto Ricans

8. Which conclusion is MOST true based on information in the above timeline?

Ⓐ Native Puerto Ricans had a majority in the island's government from the beginning of their time as a U.S. territory

Ⓑ Spanish was declared the official language of Puerto Rico, even though the island became a U.S. territory

Ⓒ Puerto Rico succumbed to U.S. expansionism but also advocated to get more rights for the island natives

Ⓓ Puerto Rico natives formed a violent revolution against U.S. colonialism

- 73 -

9. The first "May Day" celebration for the rights of working people occurred in the U.S. on May 1, 1886, with more than 300,000 workers across the country participating in a one-day strike. Which factor below BEST describes one cause of this historic event?

Ⓐ Government policies on Native Americans meant that this group was assimilating into groups of workers, but they were also causing agitation among workers.

Ⓑ By 1886, union membership had grown to a high point, such as with a group called Knights of Labor having a membership of one million workers.

Ⓒ A law passed in 1885 raising an income tax on working people had caused a lot of anger among average workers.

Ⓓ Immigrants from European countries brought the May Day tradition from their countries to U.S. workers.

10. Which of the following was one of the terms in the Treaty of Versailles at the end of World War I?

Ⓐ Germany had lands in Europe taken away but was able to keep their overseas colonies.

Ⓑ The German army was reduced but they were allowed to keep tanks.

Ⓒ Germany had to admit full responsibility for starting the war.

Ⓓ Germany was allowed to unite with Austria.

Use the excerpt and your knowledge of social studies to answer the following question:

From The Jungle, by Upton Sinclair, 1906

"The packers had secret mains, through which they stole billions of gallons of the city's water. The newspapers had been full of this scandal—once there had even been an investigation, and an actual uncovering of the pipes; but nobody had been punished, and the thing went right on. And then there was the condemned meat industry, with its endless horrors. The people of Chicago saw the government inspectors in Packingtown, and they all took that to mean that they were protected from diseased meat; they did not understand that these hundred and sixty-three inspectors had been appointed at the request of the packers, and that they were paid by the United States government to certify that all the diseased meat was kept in the state."

11. After President Theodore Roosevelt read "The Jungle," he ordered an investigation of the meat packing industry. What else MOST likely was a result of the book and the investigation?

Ⓐ Upton Sinclair ran a successful campaign to become the first Socialist congressional representative from New Jersey

Ⓑ Upton Sinclair published several other books that were just as commercially successful as "The Jungle" was

Ⓒ Theodore Roosevelt announced that he agreed with Upton Sinclair's political philosophy of socialism

Ⓓ Congress passed a "Pure Food and Drugs Act" and a "Meat Inspection Act" in 1906

Use the newspaper image and your knowledge of social studies to answer the following question:

12. Which amendment is referenced in this newspaper headline?

Ⓐ 16th Amendment

Ⓑ 17th Amendment

Ⓒ 18th Amendment

Ⓓ 19th Amendment

13. Harry Laughlin, a scientist and eugenicist, testified in Congressional hearings on immigration policies in the early 1920s that immigrants from some European countries were biologically inferior to native-born white Americans. Laughlin claimed that immigrants had lower intelligence test scores and higher rates of criminal activity. What was one result of such eugenicist theories?

Ⓐ The Johnson Act was passed by Congress in 1924 to restrict annual immigration from certain regions of Europe

Ⓑ Congress passed an act in 1923 to increase the numbers of prisons in cities with high immigrant populations

Ⓒ The eugenics theories led believers in 1925 to form their own political party known as the Populists

Ⓓ Ellis Island closed in 1925 and no longer processed any immigrants into the U.S.

14. In 1918, Marcus Garvey started a newspaper in the U.S. called *The Negro World*, which promoted Garvey's philosophy of black pride, self-help, and economic independence for African Americans and Africans anywhere in the world. What other movement in the 1920s could be said to have been influenced by Marcus Garvey's ideas?

Ⓐ Accommodation

Ⓑ Black Panthers

Ⓒ Social Darwinism

Ⓓ Harlem Renaissance

Use the timeline and your knowledge of social studies to answer the following question:
Aggressions by Dictators in 1930s to early 1940s

1936　Italy (under Benito Mussolini) attacked and took over Ethiopia

1938　Germany (under dictator Adolf Hitler) took over Austria

1939　Hitler invaded Poland

15. Which event could be added to this timeline to show the final cause for Americans entering into World War II?

Ⓐ 1939　Japan entered an alliance with Germany and Italy

Ⓑ 1940　Germany invaded France

Ⓒ 1940　Germany invaded Denmark and Norway

Ⓓ 1941　Fascist government in Japan bombed Pearl Harbor

- 76 -

Use the excerpt and your knowledge of social studies to answer the following question:
"Project TRINITY was the name given to the war-time effort [in the United States] to produce the first nuclear detonation. A plutonium-fueled implosion device was detonated on 16 July 1945 at the Alamogordo Bombing Range in south-central New Mexico."
-from Project Trinity 1945-1946, by Carl Maag and Steve Rohrer

16. Why was Project Trinity a very important program for the U.S. during World War II?

Ⓐ The U.S. wanted to use nuclear energy to power their factories in helping the war effort.

Ⓑ Germany and Japan both had programs to build an atomic bomb, so the U.S. needed one first to win the war.

Ⓒ Italy and Germany both had plans to build an atomic bomb, so the U.S. needed to build one before their enemies did.

Ⓓ The U.S. wanted to use the threat of a nuclear bomb to put down any insurrections that might start in Japanese internment camps in New Mexico.

Use the list and your knowledge of social studies to answer the following question:
Around 160,000 Allied troops landed along a 50-mile stretch of French coastline to fight Nazi Germany.
More than 5,000 ships and 13,000 aircraft gave support for the Allied attack.

17. Which World War II battle does the above information describe?

Ⓐ D-day, the Normandy Invasion

Ⓑ Battle of the Bulge

Ⓒ Battle of Midway

Ⓓ Battle of Britain

Use the photograph and your knowledge of social studies to answer the following question:

Some victory gardeners displaying their vegetables 1942 or 1943

18. What was one main purpose of a Victory Garden in the U.S. during World War II?

Ⓐ To ensure that the domestic food supply was not being poisoned by foreign spies or infiltrators

Ⓑ To decrease demand on commercial vegetable growers, making more food available to soldiers

Ⓒ To provide more nutritious food for poor immigrant populations

Ⓓ To sell grown foods at markets and raise money for war bonds

Use the map and your knowledge of social studies to answer the following question:

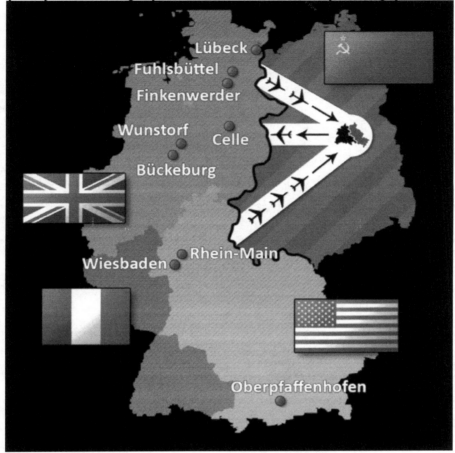

Post World War II Germany, around 1948-49, showing Germany divided into the American sector, British sector, French sector, and Russian sector. The capital city of Berlin was also divided into those four sectors after the war.

19. This map shows political divisions of Germany after World War II. What else does this map illustrate with the use of arrows?

    Ⓐ The area designated as "free airspace" where travelers from the different sectors could travel in between East and West Germany

    Ⓑ The "Berlin Bombing" routes used by Allied aircraft to bomb enemy targets in East Berlin that were under control of the U.S.S.R.

    Ⓒ The "Berlin Airlift," the routes used by Allied aircraft to airlift supplies to West Berlin because the Soviet Union was imposing a blockade on supplies to West Berlin

    Ⓓ The plans for moving Germany's defeated air force and airplanes in between new airports owned by Soviet, American, French, and British governments

Use the list and your knowledge of social studies to answer the following question:
- Communist North Korea invaded South Korea in 1950.
- President Truman worried that the Soviet Union and China planned to expand communism throughout Asia.
- The United Nations passed a resolution in 1950 urging United Nations member countries to give assistance to South Korea in their battle against North Korea.

20. What would be the BEST title for this list that summarizes what all of the items on the list have in common?

Ⓐ Reasons Why the Policy of Containment was Ineffective

Ⓑ Reasons for United States Involvement in the Korean War

Ⓒ Reasons for the Popularity of McCarthyism in the United States

Ⓓ Reasons Why the House Un-American Activities Committee Formed

21. In 1969, President Nixon made a speech about the Vietnam War and referred to a "silent majority" of Americans. Which Americans did he define as the "silent majority"?

Ⓐ Americans who were against the Vietnam War but were not actively protesting in the streets.

Ⓑ Americans who supported the Vietnam War but were not overly expressive about their opinions, unlike certain loud war protestors.

Ⓒ American troops who had returned from fighting in the Vietnam War in need of social services, even though they did not loudly demand such services.

Ⓓ American politicians who were quietly listening to opinions about the Vietnam War from their constituents before making any political decisions about the war.

Use the excerpt and your knowledge of social studies to answer the following question:
The Black Experience in America by Norman Coombs, 1972
"During Reconstruction blacks played a significant political role throughout the South. Besides voting in large numbers, they were elected to local, state, and federal offices. Between 1869 and 1901, two became U. S. Senators and twenty were members of the House of Representatives. Senators Revels and Bruce were elected from Mississippi. P. B. S. Pinchback was elected to the Senate from Louisiana, but he was not permitted to take his seat. He did serve as Lieutenant Governor of Louisiana, and, for three days, was Acting Governor."

22. Which amendment MOST made the above events possible?

Ⓐ 13th Amendment

Ⓑ 14th Amendment

Ⓒ 15th Amendment

Ⓓ 19th Amendment

Use the chart and your knowledge of social studies to answer the following question:
<u>Chart—Percentage of African Americans in Certain Military Ranks, 1964-1966</u>

Rank E-6 (Staff Sergeant or Petty Officer, First Class)			
	1964	1965	1966
Army	13.9	15.5	18.1
Navy	4.7	5.0	5.6
Marine Corps	5.0	5.3	10.4

Source: Office, Deputy Assistant Secretary of Defense (Civil Rights)

23. In the early 1960s, President Kennedy became more committed to helping civil rights causes, including the cause of desegregation in the military. Based on this chart, what conclusion about African Americans in 1964-66 military ranks can be made?

Ⓐ African Americans started making up a larger percentage of Major or Lieutenant Commander Ranks in the Army, Navy, and Marines

Ⓑ African Americans started making up a larger percentage of Staff Sergeant or Petty Officer Ranks in the Army, Navy, and Marines

Ⓒ African Americans started making up a larger percentage of Staff Sergeant or Petty Officer Ranks in the Army and Marines, but not in the Navy.

Ⓓ The percentage of African-American Staff Sergeants or Petty Officers grew between 1954 and 1965, but then declined again between 1965 and 1966

24. Which part of the Iran-Contra affair (that took place under President Reagan in the 1980s) consisted of illegal activities?

Ⓐ The U.S. convinced other countries to sell weapons to Iran. The Contras inside the Nicaraguan government also sold weapons to Iran.

Ⓑ Iran was allowed to begin research into nuclear weapons. Contras fighting the government in Nicaragua were allowed to buy weapons from Iran.

Ⓒ Weapons were illegally sold to Iran by the U.S. government. Funds from the arms sales were illegally diverted to support the Contras, a group fighting the Nicaraguan government.

Ⓓ The U.S. sold weapons to the Contras, a group supporting the Nicaraguan government. Funds from the arms sales were illegally diverted to a group inside Iran fighting that government.

Use the excerpt and your knowledge of social studies to answer the following question:
"America is at war with a transnational terrorist movement fueled by a radical ideology of hatred, oppression, and murder. Our National Strategy for Combating Terrorism, first published in February 2003, recognizes that we are at war and that protecting and defending the Homeland, the American people, and their livelihoods remains our first and most solemn obligation."
From *National Strategy for Combating Terrorism*, Sept. 2006

25. What was another name for the "National Strategy for Combating Terrorism"?

Ⓐ Homeland Radicalism

Ⓑ Persian Gulf War

Ⓒ Terrorism Crisis

Ⓓ War on Terror

Use the excerpt and your knowledge of social studies to answer the following question:
"There is a time to every purpose under the heaven--a time of war and a time of peace." So spoke one of Woodstock's most famous sons, the Reverend John Peter Gabriel Muhlenberg, in the Lutheran Church one Sunday morning after the Declaration of Independence had been issued. After delivering an inspired sermon taken from this text in which he reviewed his stand on liberty, he dramatically cast off his black pulpit robes and revealed to his astonished congregation his colonel's uniform of the Revolutionary army."

26. The excerpt describes two careers that John Peter Muhlenberg had before and during the Revolutionary War period. What were those two careers, and what third career did he have after the Revolutionary War?

Ⓐ Reverend, British Army Colonel, first Governor of Virginia

Ⓑ Speaker, British Army soldier, first Governor of Connecticut

Ⓒ Reverend, Continental Army Colonel, member of the first U.S. Congress

Ⓓ Writer, signer of the Declaration of Independence, Continental Army soldier

27. What was the primary purpose of the Chinese Exclusion Act passed by the U.S. Congress in 1882?

Ⓐ To ban Chinese from immigrating to the U.S.

Ⓑ To exclude Chinese Americans from joining unions in the U.S.

Ⓒ To ban Chinese Americans from working on railroads in the U.S.

Ⓓ To exclude Chinese from claiming settlement lands in the western U.S.

Use the photo and your knowledge of social studies to answer the following question:

Alvan Macauley (left), President of the Packard Motor Car Co. and Col. Charles A. Lindbergh with the original Packard diesel-powered Stinson "Detroiter" in the background, 1929. (Smithsonian photo A48319D.)

28. Besides flying some of the original diesel-powered airplanes, what was another notable contribution of Colonel Charles A. Lindbergh to 1920s U.S. history?

Ⓐ He made the first solo nonstop flight across the Atlantic Ocean in 1927.

Ⓑ He made the first solo nonstop flight across the Pacific Ocean in 1928.

Ⓒ He trained Amelia Earhart, the first female solo pilot, in piloting skills.

Ⓓ After Lindbergh's son was kidnapped, Congress passed the "Lindbergh Law," which made kidnapping a federal offense if a child was taken across state lines.

Use the chart and your knowledge of social studies to answer the following question:

The only unbroken code in modern military history used Native-American words for military words, but words were not direct translations. The Native-American words were for something similar to the military term being described, for example:

Native American word:	Translation:	Code for:
chay-da-gahi	Tortoise	Tank
gini	Chicken hawk (a bird that dives on its prey).	Dive bomber
ne-he-mah	Our mother	America

29. What was the name of the U.S. Marines group that used this code, and in which war was it used to communicate securely and save lives?

Ⓐ Navajo Code Talkers, World War I

Ⓑ Navajo Code Talkers, World War II

Ⓒ Sioux Secret Coders, World War I

Ⓓ Sioux Secret Coders, World War II

30. Although pressured to take military action by some advisors, President John F. Kennedy prevailed in his 1962 strategy of getting the Soviet Union to end the construction of bases for nuclear missiles on an island in return for a U.S. promise to not invade that island. Those "13 Days in October" are more famously known by what name?

Ⓐ Dominican Republic Nuclear Danger

Ⓑ Dominican Republic at the Brink

Ⓒ Cuban Communist Crisis

Ⓓ Cuban Missile Crisis

Use the excerpt and your knowledge of social studies to answer the following question:
"The animals which are found west of the Missouri River, especially in the Rocky Mountains, and far beyond them, are the buffalo, elk, deer, cimarron bear, mountain sheep, antelope, coyote, prairie-dog, etc.

The buffalo, which affords good beef to the Indian hunters, and has fed many thousand toilers over the plains to Salt Lake and California, is mainly known to boys in the comfortable buffalo robes, which everyone knows the use of in sleigh-riding. But to us officers and soldiers on the plains they are life-preservers almost, in our sleeping out nights on the ground, far away from home and good beds and blankets."

From *Three Years on the Plains* by Edmund B. Tuttle, 1870

31. Based on this excerpt, which statement would be MOST likely true about whites' settlement of the Great Plains in the late 1800s?

Ⓐ Like the Native Americans of the Great Plains, white settlers also came to rely on buffalo for food and for providing warm robes on cold nights

Ⓑ In the Great Plains there were many animals that could provide food for new white settlers, but there were not any dangerous animals

Ⓒ The white settlers came to rely on buffalo for providing food and on elk and deer for use in sleigh-riding

Ⓓ The white settlers in the Great Plains came to rely on buffalo for food, but not for any other purpose

Use the map and your knowledge of social studies to answer the following question:

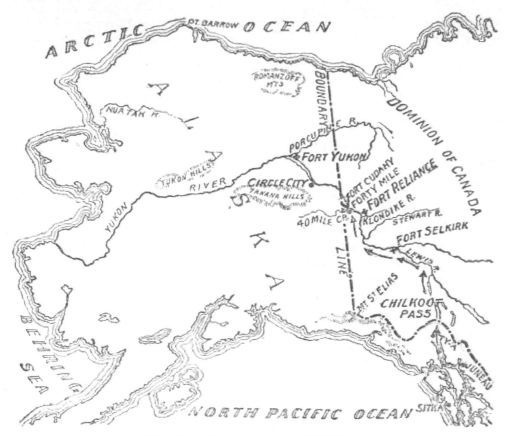

MAP OF THE YUKON GOLD DIGGINGS

32. In the 1890s, gold was discovered in the Klondike area of Alaska, and a rush of settlers came to the area. Based on the map, which of the following is MOST likely the correct order and route of how miners traveled in the area?

Ⓐ Miners buy supplies in Juneau, pack their loads and hike through Chilkoot Pass, take boats down Lewis River to the Klondike River, hike from the river to the Yukon Hills

Ⓑ Miners buy supplies in Juneau, ride on steamboats to Ty-a, pack their loads and hike through Chilkoot Pass, take boats down Lewis River to the Klondike River

Ⓒ Miners hike through the Chilkoot Pass, take boats down Lewis River to the Klondike River, buy supplies at the town of Forty Mile, pack their loads and hike forty miles into Canada

Ⓓ Miners hike through the Chilkoot Pass, take boats down Lewis River to the Klondike River, walk along that river bank to Circle City, buy supplies at Circle City

Use the excerpt and your knowledge of social studies to answer the following question:

> "At Panama earthquakes are few and unimportant, while the Nicaraguan route passes over a well-known coastal weakness. Only five disturbances of any sort were recorded at Panama, all very slight, while similar official records at San Jose de Costa Rica, near the route of the Nicaragua Canal, show for the same period fifty shocks, a number of which were severe."
>
> And later he continued: "The situation being, then, that the danger from volcanoes at Panama is nothing, and that from earthquakes practically nothing, while at Nicaragua the canal would be situated in one of the most dangerous regions of the world from both these causes, the question should be considered settled."

33. Based on this excerpt, which statement would be MOST likely true about the Panama Canal?

Ⓐ When considering where to build a canal in Central America, factors such as earthquakes and volcanoes needed to be taken into consideration.

Ⓑ It was risky to build a canal in Panama because of possible volcanoes there, but the risk of earthquakes in Nicaragua was greater.

Ⓒ There were never any volcanoes or earthquakes in Nicaragua, so there was no danger to building a canal there.

Ⓓ There were never any volcanoes or earthquakes in Panama, so there was no danger to building a canal there.

Use the excerpt and your knowledge of social studies to answer the following question:
"Some say that they left the South on account of injustice in the courts, unrest, lack of privileges, denial of the right to vote, bad treatment, oppression, segregation or lynching. Others say that they left to find employment, to secure better wages, better school facilities, and better opportunities to toil upward."

34. What would be the BEST summary of this excerpt?

Ⓐ Causes of Confederate Soldiers Abandoning the South

Ⓑ Effects of Migration from the Rust Belt to the Sun Belt

Ⓒ Causes of the Great Migration

Ⓓ Effects of Western Expansion

35. A study in 1998 found that new immigrants to the U.S. tended to settle in the "port-of-entry" states where they first entered the United States. How would this fact MOST likely affect demographics within the U.S.?

Ⓐ There would be a high number of immigrants settling in states such as California, New York, and Texas

Ⓑ There would be a high number of immigrants settling in states such as Colorado, Utah, and Nebraska

Ⓒ Native-born Americans would leave the states where new immigrants were settling

Ⓓ It would have no effect on demographics within the United States

36. Tin Pan Alley referred to the location in New York City of popular music publishers, and also to the kind of music being produced there in the 1890s and early 20th century. What were one negative impact and one positive impact of Tin Pan Alley?

Ⓐ *Positive:* Tin Pan Alley was the birthplace of American popular music and created the ASCAP (American Society of Composers, Authors, and Publishers).
Negative: ASCAP was a predominantly white group for many years until the popularity of music by African Americans arose in the late 1920s.

Ⓑ *Positive*: Tin Pan Alley sold millions of copies of sheet music.
Negative: The Tin Pan Alley location still has many music publishers but has become a high-crime area.

Ⓒ *Positive:* Tin Pan Alley gave a lot of jobs to new immigrants.
Negative: All the money earned went to publishing companies, while composers stayed poor.

Ⓓ *Positive*: Sheet music could now be sold to the public, instead of just to professional performers.
Negative: Tin Pan Alley did not hire any immigrants.

Use the list and your knowledge of social studies to answer the following question:

Disneyland
Hollywood movies
McDonald's restaurants
Pop music
Television shows

37. Which heading would BEST describe something that the items on this list have in common?

Ⓐ Things That Began in the 1920s

Ⓑ Things That Began in the 1930s

Ⓒ Things That Are Headquartered in California

Ⓓ American Pop Culture Influences on the World

Use the illustration and your knowledge of social studies to answer the following question:

Group of Converted Indians with their Pastor

38. This illustration BEST gives an example of which historical process?

Ⓐ Migration of Native Americans to Reservations

Ⓑ Movement to Assimilate Native Americans into American Culture

Ⓒ Native American Battles with White Settlers

Ⓓ Evangelicals Within the Native American Community

Use the excerpt and your knowledge of social studies to answer the following question:
A famous woman social worker wrote this in her book about her work in 1910:
"In spite of these flourishing clubs for children early established at Hull-House, and the fact that our first organized undertaking was a kindergarten, we were very insistent that the Settlement should not be primarily for the children, and that it was absurd to suppose that grown people would not respond to opportunities for education and social life."

39. Which famous woman did social work at Hull House in Chicago in the early 1900s and wrote that excerpt?

Ⓐ Susan B. Anthony

Ⓑ Jane Addams

Ⓒ Dr. Aletta Jacobs

Ⓓ Frances Willard

40. Which woman won an Outstanding Labor Leader Award for her lifetime work with Cesar Chavez on behalf of migrant farm workers in the U.S.?

Ⓐ Isabelle Allende

Ⓑ Gloria Anzaldua

Ⓒ Dolores Huerta

Ⓓ Sonia Sotomayor

41. The Great Seal of the United States that was first used in 1782 included the motto *E Pluribus Unum*. The same motto appeared on federal coins in 1795. What is the meaning of this motto?

Ⓐ In God We Trust

Ⓑ In Union We Trust

Ⓒ Out of Many, One

Ⓓ The Many are United

42. In 1997, President Clinton presented the Congressional Medal of Honor to Vernon J. Baker, a 78-year-old African American, for his courage and leadership in attacks on the enemy in Italy during a previous war. Racial prejudice during the time of this war had prevented Baker from receiving the award previously. In which war did Vernon Baker bravely fight?

Ⓐ World War I

Ⓑ World War II

Ⓒ Korean War

Ⓓ Vietnam War

43. President Franklin Roosevelt's New Deal legislation included retirement income for elderly, farm subsidies, insurance for bank deposits, public works projects, benefits for the unemployed, and more. What kind of historic change did such programs represent?

Ⓐ It was the first time that federal legislation affected farmers

Ⓑ It was the first time that the Supreme Court had the final authority to approve legislation

Ⓒ The programs gave state and federal governments increased power to affect the economy

Ⓓ The programs gave more power to state governments but took away power from the federal government.

44. The Ethics in Government Act of 1978 required elected public officials to make public some of their financial information. What could be considered a source of public demand for increased ethics in government at that time period?

Ⓐ The Watergate Scandal of the early 1970s had eroded some public trust in government officials.

Ⓑ The Teapot Dome Scandal of the late 1960s had eroded some public trust in government officials.

Ⓒ Newspapers had been making up stories in the early 1970s about public officials misusing government money.

Ⓓ Gerald Ford was not considered an ethical president, which was also the main reason he did not get re-elected to a second term.

45. Providing increased border patrols at the U.S.-Canada border was a provision of which legislation?

Ⓐ USA PATRIOT Act of 2001

Ⓑ Trade Act of 2002

Ⓒ Protection of Lawful Commerce in Arms Act of 2005

Ⓓ Secure Fence Act of 2006

46. Which statement below could be considered an advantage of the United States participating in the United Nations organization?

Ⓐ The United Nations does not involve itself in deadly conflicts or civil wars.

Ⓑ The United Nations has different foreign policy objectives than the United States has.

Ⓒ The United Nations has been a leader in helping to end the humanitarian and military crisis in Darfur.

Ⓓ The United Nations does not deal with relief for victims of natural disasters, thereby saving money for the United States.

47. In *Bush v. Gore*, the Supreme Court ruled 5-4 that a recount in that year's presidential election must take place by midnight of December 12th, 2000. The ruling came hours before the deadline, making it too late for a recount to actually occur. What is the BEST way to describe the historical aspect of this Supreme Court case?

Ⓐ This case caused states to make drastic changes in the ways that they supervised recounts in federal elections.

Ⓑ This case made history as the first time that a U.S. President had his name and cause appear in a Supreme Court case.

Ⓒ This case showed for the first time that presidential candidates needed to hire lawyers even before their campaigns started.

Ⓓ This case marked the first time that the judicial branch of government involved itself in a federal election, and critics said that the Supreme Court rather than the electorate had determined the winner of a presidential election.

48. In 1954, the Supreme Court's *Brown v. Board of Education* decision declared that school segregation and the "separate but equal" doctrine was unconstitutional. What happened afterward in southern states that same year?

Ⓐ Southern states immediately started planning how to desegregate their schools.

Ⓑ The Cold War started and everyone ignored the school desegregation movement for a few years.

Ⓒ The President immediately got involved in helping to desegregate schools in southern states, and he called in National Guard troops to assist.

Ⓓ Southern opponents of segregation used intimidation and violence against desegregation proponents, and many southern school districts avoided compliance with the new law.

49. In 1973's *White v. Regester* Supreme Court case, the court ruled that Texas county, city council, and school board districts should have elections so that members would be voted in from individual electoral districts. What kind of system did Texas have before this Supreme Court decision?

Ⓐ A vote by mail system that was full of fraud problems.

Ⓑ A voting system that allowed too many "write-in" candidates.

Ⓒ A poll tax that discouraged voters from poor districts from voting.

Ⓓ An "at large" voting system that had weakened minority voting power.

Use the excerpt and your knowledge of social studies to answer the following question:
"Mr. Rockefeller wished me to join his board and this I did. Cooperation was soon found to be much to our mutual advantage, and we now work in unison."

50. Along with John D. Rockefeller, the industrialist who wrote the above quote in his autobiography was also one of the founders of corporate philanthropy in the 20th century. He donated to libraries, schools, universities, and former employees. Who was this wealthy industrialist?

Ⓐ Henry Ward Beecher

Ⓑ Andrew Carnegie

Ⓒ Elbert H. Gary

Ⓓ John Stuart Mill

51. During World War II, Japanese Americans in internment camps were denied the right to be brought before a court to challenge the legality of their imprisonment. This was a violation of which constitutional right?

(A) Right against involuntary servitude

(B) Right to habeas corpus

(C) Right to assemble

(D) Right to vote

52. Which of the following methods was NOT used by suffragettes in their attempt to get the 19th Amendment (allowing women the right to vote) passed?

(A) Marches

(B) Nonviolent protests

(C) Speeches and written articles

(D) Payments to key senators to help the cause

53. The "laissez-faire" economists of the late 1800s, before Progressives had more influence, believed that businesses were best regulated by which entity?

(A) Federal government

(B) State or local governments

(C) Trust-busting laws

(D) Marketplace forces

Use the list and your knowledge of social studies to answer the following question:
- Provided that shipping rates should be fair and reasonable
- Required that rate information be made public
- Outlawed secret rebates
- Made price discrimination against small markets illegal
- Promised investigation of any rate abuses

54. The above list shows provisions of which piece of legislation?

(A) Pacific Railway Act of 1862

(B) Interstate Commerce Act of 1887

(C) Dollar Diplomacy Act of 1911

(D) Federal Reserve Act of 1913

55. When President Warren Harding called for a "Return to Normalcy" in 1920, the BEST summary of what he meant would be...

Ⓐ A return to the high employment rate that had dominated the U.S. during World War I

Ⓑ A return to peaceful times and a focus on domestic issues, as opposed to a focus on international war

Ⓒ A return to a period of high immigration rates that were contributing to a diverse culture and growing economy in the U.S.

Ⓓ A return to finding more territories, such as Puerto Rico and Guam acquired during the Spanish-American War, for expanding U.S. markets

Use the excerpt and your knowledge of social studies to answer the following question:
  <u>From President Herbert Hoover's State of the Union Address, December 1931</u>
    "Our people have a right to a banking system in which their deposits shall be safeguarded and the flow of credit less subject to storms. The need of a sounder system is plainly shown by the extent of bank failures. I recommend the prompt improvement of the banking laws. Changed financial conditions and commercial practices must be met. "

56. Why did President Herbert Hoover feel the need to address bank failures during his 1930 State of the Union address?

Ⓐ Bank failures were one of the causes of the Great Depression.

Ⓑ Bank failures were one of the effects of the Great Depression.

Ⓒ Hoover planned a Federal Deposit Insurance Program to insure banks against future failures.

Ⓓ The 1930 Congress planned a Federal Deposit Insurance Program to insure banks against future failures.

57. President Franklin D. Roosevelt said his New Deal programs would use the authority of the federal government to help all classes and groups of people in the country. Who was one opponent of the New Deal programs, and why?

Ⓐ *The American public*: they felt the programs were not helping enough, and a majority planned to not re-elect President Roosevelt.

Ⓑ *Herbert Hoover*: he felt the federal government should not assume so much responsibility or deficit spending.

Ⓒ *1933 Congress*: they did not pass the New Deal programs proposed by the President.

Ⓓ *1935 Congress*: they did not pass the "Second Hundred Days" New Deal programs proposed by the President.

Use the chart and your knowledge of social studies to answer the following question:

New Deal Program	How it Worked	How it Still Affects People Today
Social Security Act of 1935	Provided pensions to elderly; benefit payments to dependent mothers, disabled children, and blind people; gave unemployment insurance.	Social Security Administration still gives benefit payments to retirees who have paid taxes during their working years. There are still programs to benefit disabled and unemployed people, too.
Federal Deposit Insurance Corporation		The FDIC is still active today to maintain banking stability and public confidence by insuring deposits, protecting consumers, and overseeing bank safety and soundness.

58. Which statement would BEST fill in the blank space on the chart, explaining how the FDIC originally worked in the 1930s?

Ⓐ Gave gold to failing banks

Ⓑ Encouraged worried Americans to withdraw their money from failing banks

Ⓒ Gave insurance on checking accounts that were not earning enough interest for customers

Ⓓ Provided deposit insurance to banks and had the authority to regulate and supervise banks

59. During World War II, unemployment in the U.S. for civilians went from 14 percent in 1940 to 1.2 percent in 1944. Which choice below BEST describes a cause and an effect of this drop in unemployment?

Ⓐ *Cause*: The internment of Japanese Americans made for less competition for factory jobs. *Effect:* Decreased the need for rationing food because more was being produced in factories.

Ⓑ *Cause:* The New Deal programs were finally helping end unemployment.
Effect: A third round of New Deal programs were passed by Congress.

Ⓒ *Cause:* Wartime economic boom expanded industrial production, with less workforce competition due to need for wartime soldiers.
Effect: Helped end the Great Depression.

Ⓓ *Cause*: Increased opportunity for women and minorities to gain employment.
Effect: There was increased racism as there was increased competition for remaining jobs.

60. In the early 1950s, the birthrate in the U.S. kept climbing steadily each year, from around 3.6 million births in 1950 to 4.3 million births in 1957. Which phrase BEST describes this post war phenomenon, and tells an effect of the phenomenon?

Ⓐ "Baby Boom," benefitted the U.S. economy and led to a greater demand for consumer products

Ⓑ "Women Quitting Work Effect," caused an increase in employment opportunities for men

Ⓒ "Soldiers Returning Effect," caused more out-of-wedlock births

Ⓓ "Baby Bust," led to decreased prosperity in the 1950s

Use the list and your knowledge of social studies to answer the following question:
- A Wilderness Protection Act saved forestland from being developed
- The Elementary and Secondary Education Act provided money for public schools
- Medicare was started to help elderly with the costs of health care
- A Housing Act provided money to build low-income housing
- Pollution controls became stronger due to the Air and Water Quality Acts
- Standards were raised for safety in consumer products
- A Food Stamp program was enacted
- Head Start's preschool programs for poor children were created
- The Corporation for Public Broadcasting was created, providing many public television and radio stations

61. All of the programs on the above list fall under what category of programs?

Ⓐ President Franklin D. Roosevelt's New Deal programs

Ⓑ President John F. Kennedy's Civil Rights programs

Ⓒ President Lyndon B. Johnson's Great Society programs

Ⓓ President Richard M. Nixon's American Welfare programs

62. When the Organization of Petroleum Exporting Countries (OPEC) declared an oil embargo against the United States from 1973 to 1974, what was an effect on the U.S. free enterprise system?

Ⓐ Car owners stocked up on gasoline.

Ⓑ Auto manufacturers in the U.S. started selling cars to European customers instead of to U.S. customers.

Ⓒ The effect on the U.S. free enterprise system was minor; the U.S. had stockpiles of oil reserves and was actively drilling for oil in Texas and Alaska.

Ⓓ The U.S. experienced inflation, economic recession, and restrictions on gasoline purchases; auto manufacturers started making smaller and more fuel-efficient cars.

63. In 1997, he was called the "richest man in America" for his approximate net worth of $37 billion, which he earned in the computer industry. He tries to keep the American Dream alive for others by philanthropically donating money to schools, libraries, and computer labs. Who is this American entrepreneur?

Ⓐ Warren Buffett

Ⓑ Bill Gates

Ⓒ Robert Johnson

Ⓓ Sam Walton

Use the excerpt and your knowledge of social studies to answer the following question:

"The foreman of a Pittsburg coal company may now stand in his subterranean office and talk to the president of the Steel Trust, who sits on the twenty-first floor of a New York skyscraper. The long-distance talks, especially, have grown to be indispensable to the corporations whose plants are scattered and geographically misplaced—to the mills of New England, for instance, that use the cotton of the South and sell so much of their product to the Middle West. To the companies that sell perishable commodities, an instantaneous conversation with a buyer in a distant city has often saved a carload or a cargo."

64. The author of this excerpt is describing the social and economic/business effects of which technological innovation?

Ⓐ Coal smelting

Ⓑ Stock ticker

Ⓒ Telegraph

Ⓓ Telephone

Use the timeline and your knowledge of social studies to answer the following question:

- 1921 - Franklin Roosevelt acquired the disease called polio and lost the use of his legs at age 39
- 1930s - Polio outbreaks became more frequent in the U.S. and public sympathy was high to help the victims
- 1938 - President Franklin Roosevelt founded the National Foundation for Infantile Paralysis (NFIP), later renamed the March of Dimes Foundation, to help fund research for a polio vaccine
- 1955 - Dr. Jonas Salk developed and tested the first successful polio vaccine

65. What is one conclusion that can be made based on this timeline?

Ⓐ Historical events and the specific needs of society can contribute to medical inventions.

Ⓑ Polio outbreaks were worse in the U.S. than in other countries in the 1920s.

Ⓒ A disease outbreak can only be prevented by the development of a vaccine.

Ⓓ Franklin Roosevelt developed the first successful polio vaccine.

Use the excerpt and your knowledge of social studies to answer the following question:
In "My Life and Work," 1922, Henry Ford wrote:
"The first step forward in assembly came when we began taking the work to the men instead of the men to the work. We now have two general principles in all operations—that a man shall never have to take more than one step, if possibly it can be avoided, and that no man need ever stoop over.

The principles of assembly are these:
(1) Place the tools and the men in the sequence of the operation so that each component part shall travel the least possible distance while in the process of finishing.
(2) Use work slides or some other form of carrier so that when a workman completes his operation, he drops the part always in the same place—which place must always be the most convenient place to his hand—and if possible have gravity carry the part to the next workman for his operation.
(3) Use sliding assembling lines by which the parts to be assembled are delivered at convenient distances."

66. What is the BEST inference that can be made based on this excerpt?

Ⓐ Henry Ford worked on assembly lines alongside his workmen.

Ⓑ The development of time-study analysis in factories led to increased inventory management.

Ⓒ The development of the assembly line method in factories led to increased worker productivity.

Ⓓ Henry Ford was mostly concerned with ergonomics in the workplace so that working men would not get hurt.

Use the timeline and your knowledge of social studies to answer the following question:

- 1978: A Teflon-coated fiberglass used in astronaut spacesuits was re-used as a roofing material for buildings and stadiums in the U.S.
- 1982: Astronauts working on the lunar surface wore liquid-cooled garments under their space suits to protect them from very hot temperatures. The garments became adapted as portable cooling systems for treatment of medical conditions like burning limbs, multiple sclerosis, and spinal injuries.
- 1995: Dr. Michael DeBakey teamed up with Johnson Space Center Engineer David Saucier to develop an artificial heart pump based on space shuttle engine fuel pumps. The heart pump they developed can supplement the left ventricle's pumping capacity in a heart.

67. What is the BEST summary of the facts presented in this timeline?

Ⓐ Technology used in space explorations can also improve the quality of life on Earth

Ⓑ Architects should study all the technologies used by engineers in space explorations

Ⓒ Doctors should study all the technologies used by engineers for space explorations

Ⓓ Space explorations are too expensive, but they do have some positive benefits also

68. The U.S.-Canada Free-Trade Agreement (FTA) of 1989 was replaced in 1994 by what?

Ⓐ North American Free Trade Agreement (NAFTA)

Ⓑ Open Trade with Canada Agreement (OTC)

Ⓒ U.S. - Canada Limited Trade Agreement (LTA)

Ⓓ U.S.-Mexico Free-Trade Agreement (UMFTA)

Answers and Explanations

1. C: It best summarizes the excerpt and shows knowledge of what else is outlined in the Declaration of Independence (grievances against England and reasons for declaring independence). Choice B would be a good guess, but the Declaration was written not because of attacks by British troops, but more because of rebellions by colonists. A student may pick choice A if they focus on the "separate but equal" clause in the excerpt, but the provision of "separate but equal" policies for African-American slaves came much later in U.S. history. A student might pick choice D if focused on the "Laws of Nature" phrase in the excerpt, but the colonists did not list such laws still connecting them to England in the Declaration.

2. C: The Populist movement arose in the U.S. in the 1890s as a grassroots political movement started by southern and western farmers to fight banks, railroads, large corporations and other "elites." "Farmers United" sounds like it could be a correct choice, given the involvement of farmers, but it is incorrect. Choice A and D are also incorrect, although the "Social Gospel" movement was active around the same time period. Entrepreneurship was also on the rise during that time period.

3. A: There has not yet been an era in U.S. History defined by a land form (for example, something like a "Rocky Mountain Era"). There was a Gold Rush era but that was not named specifically for a land form. So A is the BEST choice. There have been eras defined by wars (Civil War Era), economic growth or failure (Roaring Twenties, Great Depression), and by social reforms (Progressive Era).

4. B: The sinking of the USS Maine happened in 1898, and the fact that America blamed Spain was a major cause of the U.S. and Spain declaring war on each other in 1898. All the other events listed did not happen in 1898, so even though they are related to the Spanish-American War, they would not be the correct answer. Choice A happened in 1895, choice C occurred in 1899, and choice D happened in 1902.

5. A: Choice D sounds like a good option, because this is something that did happen, but it happened before the Dawes Act. The Nez Perce conflict of 1877 also occurred before the Dawes Act, so choice C is incorrect. Choice B was the hope of Dawes and other American politicians who planned the act in order to try to help "assimilate" Native Americans, but that was not the practical result as much as choice A, the taking over of reservation lands away from Native Americans.

6. B: Railroads did not have to pay higher wages to employees until after employees started unionizing in later years. For example, in the 1880s, they were still paying low wages to Chinese railway laborers. Choice B is the best answer: raw materials and markets were better connected for the distribution of economic products. Railroad companies probably did not see a big decrease in paying taxes, and probably had to pay more taxes to the various local governments where their tracks now ran through. States and territories became better connected by railroads, so "increased competition" would not be the best answer, either.

7. A: Mahan was correctly predicting that U.S. expansionism would increase in the 1890s as Americans increasingly turned their interests "outward," and not just inward to their own country. The country's entry into WWI would not come until the early 1900s, so that answer is incorrect. Western expansion mostly occurred before the 1890s and would still be looking "inward" at their own country, even though looking to expand settlements. Census bureau counts did increase in the 1890s, but that again is concerned with the U.S. looking "inward," examining their own population, rather than looking outward to expand into other countries.

8. C: The timeline facts show that Puerto Rico did succumb to U.S. expansionism by becoming a territory, but also that native islanders fought for more political rights. There was no major violent revolution against the U.S. in those years, and no minor ones are mentioned in the timeline, so that conclusion cannot be made. Spanish was not made the official language; English and Spanish were "co-official" for a time, and then English was made official in 1917. Also, languages are not mentioned in the timeline facts. Native Puerto Ricans did not have a majority in the island's government from the beginning of their time as a U.S. territory; that did not occur until 1914 (according to the timeline facts).

9. B: It is the only answer that relates to the growth of union membership in the late 1800s, and how this had a causal relationship to the first U.S. May Day celebration in 1886 of a massive one day strike. The other statements are all false. Choice D might be a good guess due to immigration at the time, but it is not the BEST choice listed for a cause of May Day

10. C: According to the Treaty of Versailles, Germany had to admit full responsibility for the war. Germany was forbidden to unite with Austria in the Treaty. The country also had lands in both Europe AND colonial lands taken away. They had to reduce their army number of soldiers and were not allowed to keep tanks anymore. So the other choices are all incorrect.

11. D: Congress did pass a Pure Food and Drugs Act and a Meat Inspection Act in 1906 after the president ordered an investigation of the meat packing industry due to being concerned with passages from "The Jungle" by Upton Sinclair (like the passage excerpt quoted). Sinclair did subsequently write other books, but they were not as commercially successful as "The Jungle," and nothing in the excerpt or question stem could support that statement, so it is not a good answer choice. Sinclair did run a campaign to become the first congressional representative from New Jersey to be a member of the Socialist Party, but he did not win. Roosevelt did not agree with Sinclair's socialist politics. Those answers should be eliminated by the student based on their general knowledge of social studies and that time period.

12. C: While the 16th, 17th, and 19th Amendments were in a similar time period as the 18th Amendment, the specific year 1919 and the reference to "being voted dry" are clues to a student who has some historical knowledge that this headline refers to the 18th Amendment. The 18th Amendment is the one prohibiting alcohol, thus the reference to becoming "dry."

13. A: It shows an effect caused by eugenics theories, which was a law restricting immigrants in 1924. But Ellis Island did not close completely until 1954 (later becoming a historic site and national park). The Populist political party was formed in the 1890s, so that answer is incorrect. Choice B sounds like it could be a result of eugenics theories but it is actually a made-up fact.

14. D: The 1920s Harlem Renaissance has been said by history professors to have been influenced by Marcus Garvey's movement of promoting black pride and black self-reliance. The Black Panthers were probably influenced by Garvey's ideas, but their movement did not begin until later in U.S. history. Accommodation was a movement promoted by leaders such as Booker T. Washington, around the same time as Garvey, but with somewhat opposite ideals from Garvey's promotion of economic independence. (Accommodation would be to interact economically with whites but accommodate to their separate but equal segregation rules.) Social Darwinism was a movement in the 1920s that could not be said to be influenced by Marcus Garvey, because most social Darwinists favored white races.

15. D: The Japanese attack on Pearl Harbor was the turning point which caused the U.S. to enter into World War II, even though the other events were all alarming to the U.S. and caused them to give financial assistance to the Allies before officially entering the war on the Allies' side. A student might guess that the alliance between Japan, Germany, and Italy was the turning point because it involves Japan becoming an Axis power, but it was the actual attack on Pearl Harbor which led to America entering the war.

16. B: Germany and Japan both had scientists working on nuclear bombs, and one of Project Trinity's most important goals was to make sure that the U.S. developed a bomb first and could thereby win the war through superior technology. Italy was not yet working on atomic bombs. A student might pick choice D because the excerpt mentions New Mexico and potential Japanese enemies, but that is incorrect. Choice A is also incorrect as the development of nuclear energy was not the goal of Project Trinity.

17. A: The "French coastline" is a clue that the Normandy Invasion is the correct answer, although a student may think "Bulge" or "Midway" is located in France. The high number of troops, ships, and aircraft is another clue that the facts describe D-Day. But a student not familiar with all of the other battles in World War II may pick one of the incorrect answers.

18. B: A main purpose of Victory Gardens was to decrease demand on commercial vegetable growers, thereby making more food available to soldiers. There were other purposes, such as providing nutritious foods to all people (not just poor immigrants) on the home front and boosting morale at home, but those were secondary and are not listed as answer choices. The other three answer choices listed are all incorrect.

19. C: The map's arrows show the routes the Berlin Airlift used to supply West Berlin with food supplies during a Soviet blockade. It does not show a bombing route, a route for moving captured German airplanes, or a route for tourists.

20. B: While all the titles have a connection of some kind to at least one or two items on the given list, choice B provides the BEST title for the list to show what all the items have in common: reasons for U.S. involvement in the Korean War. The policy of containment may have been partially effective, because Korea was only one country falling to communism. The United Nations item would probably not fall under a title about containment, McCarthyism, or the HUAC committee, because those were all more internal to the U.S. only. The U.N. was encouraging nations to get involved in the Korean War, so it fits under that title.

21. B: When Nixon referred to a "silent majority," he meant Americans who supported the Vietnam War but were not overly expressive about their opinions, unlike certain loud war

- 103 -

protestors. The other options all relate to Americans and their relations to or opinions about the Vietnam War, but none of those are correct answers for the meaning of a "silent majority."

22. C: While the 13th and 14th Amendments granted important freedom from slavery and citizenship to African Americans, it was the 15th Amendment, a voting rights amendment, which made it possible for African Americans to elect each other as representatives by voting in large numbers. The 19th Amendment was also a voting rights amendment, but for women, and after the time period described in the excerpt.

23. B: This item tests the student's knowledge of armed forces desegregation AND the student's ability to read a chart. Reading the chart correctly and knowing general civil rights history will tell the student that choice B is correct. African Americans started making up a larger percentage of Staff Sergeant or Petty Officer Ranks in the Army, Navy, and Marines. If the student reads the type of officer rank incorrectly on the chart, he or she might pick choice A. The percentage of African-American staff sergeants and petty officers in the Navy did not increase as much as in the Army or Marines, so a student might pick C, but there was still a slight increase, making choice C incorrect. Choice D is incorrect if the student understands the "years" columns in the charts.

24. C: It is the only choice that states what constituted illegal activities because they violated an arms embargo that was in place against Iran, and was an illegal diversion of funds. Weapons were illegally sold to Iran by the U.S. government. Funds from the arms sales were illegally diverted to support the Contras, a group fighting the Nicaraguan government. The other answer choices offer incorrect variations on these statements, or confuse the fact that Contras were against and not inside the Nicaraguan government.

25. D: The "War on Terror" is the correct terminology. "Homeland Radicalism" takes some words from the excerpt but does not describe how the U.S. was combating terrorism. The Persian Gulf War may have been one part of the War on Terror, but it does not include homeland security measures. The phrase "Terrorism Crisis" may have been used by the media or government at some point, but not as often as "War on Terror."

26. C: The excerpt gives information that Muhlenberg was a reverend and then a colonel in the Continental Army (as shown by his revealing of a Revolutionary colonel's uniform). The third correct choice is that he was one of the members of the first U.S. Congress, which the student should know from general social studies knowledge (as it is not in the excerpt). Or at least the student could use process of elimination to eliminate some of the other incorrect answers that claim he was first Governor of Connecticut or Virginia, a signer of the Declaration of Independence, or a British Army member.

27. A: The Chinese Exclusion Act of 1882 was passed for the purpose of banning Chinese immigrants from the United States. Students with knowledge of social issues affecting immigrants during that time period will know this answer. Choices C and D (prohibiting Chinese Americans from working on railroads or settling in the west) were probably secondary purposes of the act, but were not written into the legislation as choice A was.

28. A: Choices C and D are good guesses, because Amelia Earhart was the first female solo pilot, but Lindbergh did not train her. His son was kidnapped and it did lead to the law passed by Congress, but not until the mid-late 1930s. He was also not the first solo pilot

- 104 -

across the Pacific in the 1920s. Choice A is correct: He was the first solo pilot to fly nonstop across the Atlantic Ocean in 1927.

29. B: The Navajo Code Talkers were the U.S. Marines group in World War II that used this code to save lives. The other choices all sound like reasonable alternatives, because tanks and dive bombers were used in World War I and II, and Sioux and Navajo were both American-Indian tribes at the time. Also, the term "code" appears in all four answer choices. But a student with general social studies knowledge at this grade level should know that B is the correct answer.

30. D: The Cuban Missile Crisis is the more famous name for the "13 Days in October" in which President John F. Kennedy played an important role. It is also sometimes called "World at the Brink," which may cause students to incorrectly choose answer B. It was a crisis involving fears of communism, which could lead students to incorrectly pick choice C. There was nuclear danger, and the Dominican Republic is another island in the Caribbean near the coast of America, which could lead students to incorrectly pick choice A. Their general knowledge of social studies at this grade level should lead to the correct choice of D.

31. A: Like the Native Americans of the Great Plains, white settlers also came to rely on buffalo for food and for providing warm robes on cold nights. The student needs to read the excerpt closely to understand that there were other uses for buffalo besides just food. A student who does not read the excerpt closely might pick choice C if he or she associated deer and elk with sleigh-riding, as many people do. A student might pick choice B if he or she considers that none of the animals listed are dangerous, though that could be a misreading because coyote, bear, and sometimes even buffalo and elk could be dangerous to settlers.

32. B: While it might be easier to buy supplies after the long hike through Chilkoot Pass, the fact was that miners would have to buy their supplies in the biggest city, Juneau, before making the rest of the trip. Also, some choices can be eliminated based on the fact that there does not seem to be a lot happening on the map at Yukon Hills or 40 miles into the Dominion of Canada. So choice B is the correct answer, which students can determine from the map, the arrows on the map, the collection of mining camps around the Klondike River, and their general knowledge of social studies: miners buy supplies in Juneau, steamboats carry them from Juneau to Ty-a, they pack their loads and hike through Chilkoot Pass, and they take boats down Lewis River to the Klondike River.

33. A: Choice D sounds possibly correct because the Senator is concluding that Panama is a superior location for a canal, but he notes that there actually were a few earthquakes in Panama, so it can't be said that there were never earthquakes in Panama. Choice A is correct that earthquake and volcano dangers to canals had to be considered when picking a location for a canal. Panama was chosen over Nicaragua because it had less earthquake risk and no volcano risk.

34. C: The excerpt gives a summary of Causes of the Great Migration. A student should know from general social studies knowledge that the Great Migration refers to movements of African Americans from southern states to states in the Northern, Western, and Midwestern United States. The excerpt gives the reasons why African Americans would make such a move. A student might pick answer A because of mention of the South (if not reading closely), or might pick the other choices for mention of migration or expansion, but only C is correct.

35. A: The fact that immigrants tended in the 1990s to settle in port-of-entry states means that, for U.S. demographics, there would be a high number of immigrants settling in states such as California, New York, and Texas. Colorado, Utah, and Nebraska are not typical port-of-entry states (even though they do have airports). The fact given does not provide any implication that native-born Americans would flee from states where new immigrants are settling. However, there is also no reason to think that there would be zero demographic effect from an influx of new immigrants, making choices C and D incorrect.

36. A: A positive impact of Tin Pan Alley was that it was the birthplace of American popular music and created the ASCAP (American Society of Composers, Authors, and Publishers). A negative about Tin Pan Alley and ASCAP was that it was a predominantly white group for many years until the late 1920s, when the popularity of blues and jazz music by African–American musicians gained them admittance into the ASCAP. For all the other choices, the positive impact listed is correct. But the negative impacts listed are all incorrect, thus making those choices all incorrect. Composers did become rich from Tin Pan Alley; the location is no longer a hub of music publishing companies today as it once was; and they did give jobs to many new immigrants, especially Jewish and Russian immigrants in NYC.

37. D: All of the items on the list represent American Pop Culture Influences on the World. Many of the list items do have headquarters in California, but McDonald's has its headquarters in Illinois. Some of the things began in the 1920s or 30s, but not all of them, so those answer choices would also be incorrect.

38. B: The illustration best shows an example of the Americanization Movement to Assimilate Native Americans into American Culture. There may have been a battle between Native Americans and white settlers before or after this illustration, but that is not shown in the picture. Native Americans did not tend to be evangelicals; rather, the white settlers were evangelical about converting Native Americans to their religion. The picture also does not detail the move of Native Americans to reservations, although that also could have become before or after the illustration shown.

39. B: Based on the fact that the excerpt mentions Hull House, and information is given that the woman was a famous social worker in Chicago in the early 1900s, the student should be able to figure out that Jane Addams is the correct answer. Dr. Jacobs was a Dutch suffragette leader who invited Addams to some international projects with her. Susan B. Anthony was also a suffragette, but in the U.S. and around the same time period as Addams. Frances Willard was a social reformer whose work was all done in the 1800s.

40. C: Dolores Huerta won the Outstanding Labor Leader Award from the state of California in 1984 recognizing her lifetime of work with Cesar Chavez on behalf of migrant farm workers. Gloria Anzaldua was a poet and cultural critic. Isabel Allende is a fiction writer from Chile. Sonia Sotomayor is the new Supreme Court Justice.

41. C: The correct translation of *E Pluribus Unum* is "Out of Many, One." "In God We Trust" was adopted as the official motto of the U.S. later in history. "In Union We Trust" might be a good guess because "Unum" sounds like it could be a Latin version of "Union." "The many are united" also sounds like a plausible translation for *E Pluribus Unum*, even though it is actually incorrect.

42. B: The fact that Baker fought in Italy is a clue that either WWI or WWII is the correct answer, and that both the Korean War and Vietnam War would be incorrect, even though there was still some racial prejudice during the times of those wars. The fact that President Clinton presented Baker with the award gives a clue that it must have been for fighting during WWII, as Baker would probably not have been old enough to fight in WWI and still be alive under President Clinton's years. In fact, a student could deduce that, if Baker was 78 years old in 1997 that would mean he was born in 1919, which was after WWI. Also, general social studies knowledge suggests that students know who Vernon J. Baker is for this grade level.

43. C: The New Deal programs gave state and federal governments increased power to affect the economy. They did not take power away from the federal government. The programs did not need Supreme Court approval to be passed, because Congress passed the New Deal. And it was also not the first time that legislation affected farmers, because there was a Federal Farm Loan act in 1916, and other laws before the mid-1930s that probably affected farmers.

44. A: The Ethics in Government Act of 1978 was enacted after the Watergate Scandal of the early 1970s had eroded some public trust in government officials. The Teapot Dome Scandal occurred much earlier in the century, not in the 1960s. Newspapers were also not making up stories about unethical government officials, but they were reporting on Watergate. It is true that Gerald Ford did not get re-elected, partly because he was unpopular for pardoning Nixon, but not because he was considered unethical. Ford was not the impetus for the Ethics Act.

45. A: Providing increased border controls on the Canada-U.S. border was part of the USA PATRIOT Act of 2001 and affected the private and public sectors of people traveling between those two countries. The other choices listed all sound like they could be related to interactions between the U.S. and Canada. For example, lawful commerce in arms could relate to guns sold between countries, but it was for guns within the United States. A Trade Act might apply to U.S.-Canada trade, but not to border patrols. The "Fence" Act applied to the Mexico-U.S. border, not the Canada-U.S. border.

46. C: The U.N. has been a leader in helping end the crisis in Darfur, which helps the U.S. and its international image when it participates in the U.N. The other choices are all false statements. The U.N. does get involved in deadly conflicts, civil wars, and aid for victims of natural disasters. The U.N. also generally does have the same foreign policy objectives as the U.S.

47. D: This case marked the first time that the judicial branch of government involved itself in a federal election, and critics said that the Supreme Court rather than the electorate had determined the winner of a presidential election. There may have been some changes in the way states did recounts, but that is not the BEST description of the historical importance of the case. Choice B is incorrect because there had been other Supreme Court cases with president's names in them, such as *U.S. v. Nixon* in 1974, and likely several others too. Also, presidential candidates had probably been hiring lawyers even before campaigns started, long before that year's election.

48. D: Southern opponents of segregation used intimidation and violence against desegregation proponents, and many southern school districts avoided compliance with the new law. The President eventually did have to call in National Guard troops to help with desegregation, but that was a few years later. The Cold War may have started in the 1950s, but did not draw complete attention away from segregation issues.

49. D: Choice A sounds like a good guess, but choice D is the correct answer. Before the *White v. Regester* Supreme Court case, Texas had an "at large" voting system that had weakened minority voting power. The new voting from individual districts would allow more equal representation for heavily Hispanic voting districts, allowing them to have more Hispanic representatives. Choice C would not be correct because the poll tax was outlawed many years before the 1973 case.

50. B: Andrew Carnegie was a wealthy industrialist who, both alone and in cooperation with John Rockefeller, gave money to schools, universities, libraries, and former employees, starting the modern practice of corporate philanthropy in the early 1900s. Henry Ward Beecher was a leader who encouraged wealthy men to donate money to good causes around the same time period. John Stuart Mill was also a contemporary of Carnegie and encouraged donations for education. Elbert H. Gary was Carnegie's partner in a steel company, but not the main impetus behind philanthropic donations. So Andrew Carnegie is the correct answer, and the excerpt is from Carnegie's autobiography.

51. B: Students who know the meaning of "right to habeas corpus" will know that it means the right to be brought before a court, which was unconstitutionally denied to Japanese Americans in internment camps during World War II. The other options are all rights which were also violated against Japanese Americans in camps, but not in this particular example of not getting a court date. A student who does not know the meaning of *habeas corpus* may be able to use process of elimination about the other rights (although they may confuse "assembling" with going to a court, or confuse "involuntary servitude" with camp "imprisonment") in order to get the correct answer.

52. D: Payments to senators were not a method used by suffragettes trying to get the 19th Amendment allowing women the right to vote passed. They did use all of the other methods, however, such as speeches, writing articles, nonviolent protesting, and marching.

53. D: It is the best description of what laissez-faire economists believed, which is that marketplace forces were enough to regulate businesses. In contrast, most Progressives wanted more trust-busting laws and federal, state, and local government intervention to help regulate businesses that were perhaps producing unsafe products, forming monopolies to drive up prices, or taking advantage of working people.

54. B: The Interstate Commerce Act of 1887 provided for all the measures listed in the table, although not all were able to be completely enforced. Reading the list carefully and having a general knowledge of social studies and U.S. history should lead students to the correct answers, although a student could mistakenly pick one of the other choices listed for their connection to railways, dollars, or Federal Reserve money. (Dollar Diplomacy was a strategy, not an actual piece of legislation.)

55. B: It is the BEST summary for what President Warren Harding meant by a "Return to Normalcy." He was calling for a return to peaceful times and a focus on domestic issues, as opposed to a focus on international war. Choice A is a good guess because the president would want a good economy, and industry had been busy during WWI before falling off slightly after the war. But choice B is the best answer. He was not calling for going out in search of more territories or for higher immigration rates.

56. A: Herbert Hoover addressed bank failures in his 1930 State of the Union address because bank failures were one of the primary causes of the Great Depression. Congress eventually did want to start a Federal Deposit Insurance Program to help insure banks against future bank failures, but that was the 1933 Congress and Franklin Roosevelt, not the 1930 Congress and Herbert Hoover.

57. B: Herbert Hoover was a main opponent of the New Deal, for the reason listed in this answer choice. The New Deal programs were passed by the 1933 Congress and again in 1935 Congress for the "Second Hundred Days" of New Deal programs. The New Deal programs proved to be popular with the American public, who overwhelmingly re-elected FDR for his second term as President, so choice A is incorrect.

58. D: It best fills in the blank space on the chart, explaining how the FDIC originally worked in the 1930s: "Provided deposit insurance to banks and had the authority to regulate and supervise banks." Seeing the chart's statement of how the FDIC still works today should give students a clue to the correct answer. The FDIC did not give gold to banks, although gold was stored and Fort Knox was built in the 1930s. A student might choose C for its mention of "insurance," but that was not the kind of insurance provided by the FDIC. Also, the FDIC was supposed to prevent customer runs on banks, not encourage them.

59. C: It gives the BEST explanation of a cause and an effect of the decrease in unemployment during WWII. Choice C states "Cause: Wartime economic boom expanded industrial production, with less workforce competition due to need for wartime soldiers. Effect: Helped end the Great Depression." Those are both true statements related to decreased unemployment during the war. All the other choices give false causes and effects. Choice D gives a cause that is really an effect of the decrease in unemployment (that women and minorities could more easily be hired).

60. A: While an argument could be made that choice B is also correct, there was not a phenomenon actually named the "Women Quitting Work Effect," so choice A is the BEST choice for describing the phenomenon illustrated by the given statistic. The statistic shows the post war Baby Boom, and its effect was to increase the economy and consumer demand for products. Choice D describes the opposite of a Baby Boom, so it is not correct, and choice C was not a historical phenomenon.

61. C: All the programs listed were part of President Lyndon B. Johnson's Great Society programs. The students' general knowledge of social studies should place most of those programs within the 1960s time period, making Presidents Kennedy or Johnson the best guesses. But because many of the programs do not have to do with civil rights, Johnson becomes the best guess for a student to make over the other choices provided.

62. D: The result of OPEC's oil embargo on the U.S. free enterprise system was inflation, economic recession, and restrictions on gasoline purchases; and auto manufacturers making smaller and more fuel-efficient cars. U.S. auto manufacturers may have sold cars to Europe also, but Europe was also targeted by OPEC's embargo. Choices A and C are also incorrect.

63. B: While all the entrepreneurs listed are also philanthropic donors, and have at times been considered one of the richest men in the world, the mention of "computer industry" will be a clue to most students with basic social studies/current events knowledge that Bill Gates is the correct answer.

64. D: The stock ticker and the telegraph could be related to the information in this excerpt because they were ways for businessmen to relay information to each other, as described in the excerpt. However, the astute student will see that the excerpt describes businessmen talking to each other, therefore the excerpt is describing the benefits of the telephone invention. A student might pick choice A, coal smelting, if they only focus on the first sentence of the excerpt about the coal company foreman.

65. A: It can BEST be made based on the timeline facts. Historical events and the specific needs of society can contribute to medical inventions, such as how the history of polio outbreaks and the fact that a President had the disease contributed to the scientific discovery of a polio vaccine. The other statements cannot be proven true by the timeline facts. Other countries besides the U.S. also had polio outbreaks in the 1920s and 1930s. Disease outbreaks can sometimes be prevented in other ways besides just from vaccines. And it was Jonas Salk, not FDR, who invented the polio vaccine, although FDR helped raise money to fund scientific research.

66. C: It is the BEST inference that can be made based on the excerpt, which discusses the new assembly line method that Ford used in factories and how it increased the productivity of workers. The development of the assembly line method in factories led to increased worker productivity. The increased productivity can be inferred from the discussion of "convenience" and lessening steps. The excerpt does not discuss time-study analysis (at least not as much as assembly lines, even if some mention of time is included), and does not discuss inventory management as much. It does not describe Ford working on the assembly line alongside his employees. While there is some mention of ergonomics (having men not have to stoop, for example), it is not the main focus of the excerpt, so would not be the BEST inference to make. Also, it could be bad ergonomics for workers to not take many steps and to repeat the same movements over and over on assembly lines.

67. A: It is the BEST summary of the facts presented in the timeline, which are that technologies used in space explorations can also improve the quality of life on Earth. It is a good suggestion that doctors and architects study space technologies, but just naming one of those professions does not summarize the whole timeline, because only one fact deals with architectural use of space technologies, and using the doctor choice as a summary leaves out the architectural use. Choice D may be a true statement, but because there is no mention of the cost of space exploration in the timeline, it is not a good summary of the timeline.

68. A: Students who know enough about North American Trade and the recent U.S. policy of involvement in such trade will know that NAFTA was started in 1994 and is the correct answer. The other three options sound like plausible replacements if a U.S.-Canada Free

Trade Agreement was being replaced, but they are not real organizations and so they are not correct answers.

Practice Test #2

Practice Questions

Use the chart and your knowledge of social studies to answer the following question:

ERA in U.S. History	Approximate Dates	Defining Characteristics of this Era
Gilded Age or Progressive Era	1890-1914	The era was called "gilded" because of expanded wealth and prosperity. "Progressive" describes the politics of the time that called for social reforms and eliminating corruption in government.
World War I Era	1914-1918	The U.S. was involved in fighting a war in Europe.
Roaring Twenties	1918-1928	
Great Depression	1929-1940	
World War II Era	1941-1945	
Cold War Era	1945-1964	

1. Which defining characteristic listed below should go in the row for describing the Roaring Twenties Era?

Ⓐ After a World War, America wanted to help rebuild Europe and prevent the Soviet Union's possible expansion of communism.

Ⓑ After the stock market crash, many businesses failed and unemployment became high.

Ⓒ The U.S. was involved in fighting a war with Allies against Germany, Japan, and Italy.

Ⓓ The economy was strong with a great demand for new products, while culture in this era, also known as the "Jazz Age," became more experimental.

2. Which Founding Father was governor of Connecticut during and after the Revolutionary War, and was the only governor of a British colony who sided with colonists during the Revolutionary War?

Ⓐ Charles Carroll

Ⓑ Benjamin Rush

Ⓒ Jonathan Trumbull

Ⓓ John Witherspoon

Use the map and your knowledge of social studies to answer the following question:

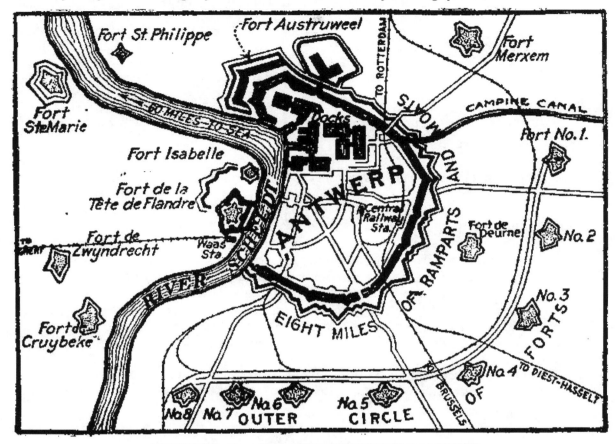

ANTWERP AND ITS FORTIFICATIONS

3. Why was the city of Antwerp in Belgium so heavily fortified in 1914?

Ⓐ World War I had started; Germany had invaded other Belgian cities and was going to invade Antwerp also.

Ⓑ World War I had started; Italy had invaded other Belgian cities and was going to invade Antwerp also.

Ⓒ Antwerp was fortifying against British air attacks that might take place during World War I.

Ⓓ Antwerp feared a Russian invasion after the start of World War I.

4. Which choice below lists some contributions to early America made by John Jay?

Ⓐ He was the first Chief Justice of New York and also a Minister to France.

Ⓑ He signed the Declaration of Independence and was one of the first mayors of New York City.

Ⓒ He served in George Washington's army during the Revolution and was Minister to Spain after the war.

Ⓓ He was a foreign minister, a contributing writer to the Federalist Papers, and an early governor of New York.

Use the excerpt and your knowledge of social studies to answer the following question:
"Perhaps the most characteristic feature of this record of lynch law for the year 1893, is the remarkable fact that five human beings were lynched and that the matter was considered of so little importance that the powerful press bureaus of the country did not consider the matter of enough importance to ascertain the causes for which they were hanged. It tells the world, with perhaps greater emphasis than any other feature of the record, that Lynch Law has become so common in the United States that the finding of the dead body of a Negro, suspended between heaven and earth to the limb of a tree, is of so slight importance that neither the civil authorities nor press agencies consider the matter worth investigating."

5. The above excerpt comes from a book written by a female African-American "muckraker" journalist and reform leader in 1895. What was this author's name?

Ⓐ Ella Baker

Ⓑ Rosa Parks

Ⓒ Sojourner Truth

Ⓓ Ida B. Wells

Use the photograph, caption, and your knowledge of social studies to answer the following question:

German Air Raiders over England
In the foreground three British planes are advancing to the attack

6. Based on the photograph and caption from a book about World War I, and your general social studies knowledge, which statement below is MOST likely true?

Ⓐ The only airplane warfare during World War I occurred over England.

Ⓑ In World War I, American allies had better airplane technology than German allies.

Ⓒ Airplane warfare was used in the Civil War before being more widely used in World War I.

Ⓓ Airplanes had their first warfare use during World War I, at first just for taking spy photographs, and later for firing guns and dropping bombs.

Use the excerpt and your knowledge of social studies to answer the following question:
In *The Great Round World and What Is Going On In It*, a weekly magazine, Sanford B. Dole was interviewed in 1898 about the U.S. plan to annex Hawaii:

> "President Dole made a glowing picture of the benefits that this country would receive from annexation. It would greatly encourage commerce between the United States and Hawaii by making the trade absolutely free, and it would open up to Americans a great many industries, the chief among them being coffee-growing.
>
> "It would also vastly improve the condition of the islands themselves.
>
> In case annexation is rejected by our Government, President Dole says the Hawaiian Government will continue much as it is at present."

7. What was Sanford B. Dole the president of in 1898?

Ⓐ The Republic of Hawaii

Ⓑ The State of Hawaii

Ⓒ The United States

Ⓓ The United States Senate

Use the list and your knowledge of social studies to answer the following question:

- It proved that the U.S. was willing to expand its empire and gain resources through imperialism (the taking of colonies).
- It allowed the U.S. to annex Guam, Hawaii, Puerto Rico, and the Philippines.
- It showed the power and strength of the U.S. army and navy.

8. What would be the BEST summarizing title for this list?

Ⓐ How the Policies of President Theodore Roosevelt Made the U.S. a World Power

Ⓑ How the Spanish-American War Helped the U.S. Become a World Power

Ⓒ How the War of 1812 Helped the U.S. Become a World Power

Ⓓ How Isolationism Led to Imperialism for the U.S.

Use the excerpt and your knowledge of social studies to answer the following question:
President Woodrow Wilson's "Fourteen Points" speech in 1918 included the following lines:

> "XIV. A general association of nations must be formed under specific covenants for the purpose of affording mutual guarantees of political independence and territorial integrity to great and small states alike.

"In regard to these essential rectifications of wrong and assertions of right we feel ourselves to be intimate partners of all the governments and peoples associated together against the Imperialists. We cannot be separated in interest or divided in

9. Based on this excerpt, what was one way that Wilson's "Fourteen Points" contrasted with his pre-war position of U.S. neutrality?

Ⓐ In 1918, Wilson agreed with the philosophy of the imperialists.

Ⓑ By 1918, Wilson thought that each nation should form its own government.

Ⓒ In this speech, Wilson believed that each nation should be able to decide its own territories.

Ⓓ In this speech, Wilson wanted to set up a League of Nations which would eventually become the United Nations.

10. Progressive Era reformers in the early 1900s wanted greater involvement by federal government in public affairs to improve schools, roads, parks, public health, farms, and more. Because government would need money for such reforms, which amendment did Progressives help pass that allowed income tax collection?

Ⓐ 16th Amendment

Ⓑ 17th Amendment

Ⓒ 18th Amendment

Ⓓ 19th Amendment

Use the illustration and your knowledge of social studies to answer the following question:

An old trench
in the Argonne near Montfaucon

A sketch from *I Was There...with the Yanks in France* by C. LeRoy Baldridge, written in 1919, shows a sketch of an old trench in the Argonne forest of France

11. Why was the Battle of the Argonne Forest in 1918 difficult and important?

Ⓐ The battle was difficult because there was no air support available to the Allies during this time and important because the Allies won anyway.

Ⓑ The battle was difficult because there were many Allied prisoners of war hidden in the trenches who needed to be rescued and important because the prisoners were rescued.

Ⓒ The battle was difficult because of the deeply forested nature of the area and important because it was the last battle won by the Germans before the end of World War I.

Ⓓ The battle was difficult because the Germans were so entrenched in this forest, having built deep trenches there, and important because it was one of the final battles of the war and helped break through Germany's western front.

12. In the Progressive Era of the late 1890s and early 1900s, political reformers wanted to make sure government represented the peoples' will. An "initiative" process began in 1898 in South Dakota and then spread to other states. Which definition BEST describes the initiative process?

Ⓐ It allowed voting citizens to give their judgment on proposed legislation before state legislators voted on the same legislation.

Ⓑ It allowed voters to gather petitions demanding special elections when they wanted to recall an unpopular public official, thereby allowing them to "un-elect" that official.

Ⓒ It allowed citizens to introduce legislation proposals at a local or state level by gathering petitions, and proposals would then be addressed by lawmakers or placed on ballots for a vote.

Ⓓ It allowed citizens to visit state legislatures and give testimony supporting a certain issue, thereby encouraging the state lawmakers to propose and pass legislation on that same issue.

13. An "Emergency Quota Law" in 1921 was signed by the president to limit new immigrants to the U.S. was most likely an effect of which popular philosophy of the time period?

Ⓐ Harlem Renaissance, which showed that African Americans had much to contribute to society and should be given jobs before letting in more immigrants.

Ⓑ Nativism, a belief that native-born Americans, especially white Americans, were superior to foreign-born Americans.

Ⓒ Prohibition, a belief that alcohol was un-American because beer was mostly brewed by German-Americans, and thus immigration of Germans and other Europeans with alcohol as part of their cultural traditions should be limited.

Ⓓ Women's Suffrage Movement, arguing that women should get rights before more immigrants were let in the U.S.

Use the timeline and your knowledge of social studies to answer the following question:
Dec. 7, 1941 - Pearl Harbor in Hawaii is bombed by Japan. The FBI arrests some Japanese-American community leaders who are held away from their families.

Dec. 8, 1941 - U.S. Congress declares war on Japan.
Feb. 19, 1942 - President Franklin D. Roosevelt signs Executive Order 9066, ordering military areas off-limits to certain people.

March 18, 1942 - President Roosevelt signs Executive Order 9102, which establishes a "War Relocation Authority."

14. What event would BEST go next in this timeline's factual sequence of events?

Ⓐ Thousands of Japanese-American men, women and children are relocated from the U.S. west coast for east coast locations.

Ⓑ All Japanese-American men are denied the chance to be U.S. soldiers for the duration of World War II.

Ⓒ Thousands of Japanese-American men, women and children are relocated to internment camps.

Ⓓ Many Japanese-American men have their passports confiscated and are forced to leave the U.S.

15. In May 1991, the First International Gathering of Children Hidden during World War II held a meeting in New York City. Around 1,600 former hidden children attended this meeting. Which of the following is the BEST explanation for why these adults had to be hidden as children in Europe during World War II?

Ⓐ They were in danger of being drafted into youth army groups in fascist Germany.

Ⓑ They were hiding from war zones and waiting for fake passports to take them to Israel.

Ⓒ They had to be hidden from French families who would have taken them away from their original homelands to adopt them.

Ⓓ They were Jewish and had to be hidden from Nazis in order to survive the Holocaust, the attempted extermination of the Jewish population by Nazi Germany.

Use the photo and your knowledge of social studies to answer the following question:

Damage Inspection: *A squadron operations officer of the 332d Fighter Group points out a cannon hole to ground crew, Italy, 1945*

16. Besides being called the "332ⁿᵈ Fighter Group," what was another name for those fighter pilots in World War II?

Ⓐ Flying Tigers

Ⓑ Red Barons

Ⓒ Top Guns

Ⓓ Tuskegee Airmen

17. Why did the North Atlantic Treaty Organization (NATO) form with a military alliance between the U.S. and several European countries in 1949?

Ⓐ It formed to defend against communist Soviet Union which had taken over some central and eastern European countries.

Ⓑ It formed to combine with the work of the United Nations in policing war-ravaged areas of the third world.

Ⓒ NATO formed to combat international terrorism and regulate nuclear weapons.

Ⓓ NATO formed to defend against a re-united Germany.

18. The "Domino Theory," first suggested by President Dwight Eisenhower but also followed by presidents after him, claimed that if one nation in Asia became a communist country, then other Asian countries would follow soon afterwards, like a set of dominoes. The U.S. fought a war in which country because of this theory?

Ⓐ Burma

Ⓑ China

Ⓒ Thailand

Ⓓ Vietnam

19. By autumn of 1967, 93 percent of American homes had a television. Most of the evening news was reporting about the Vietnam War, and about 50 million Americans watched the news each night. What was an effect of these media developments?

Ⓐ The views of war action inspired many men to register for the draft.

Ⓑ Positive media coverage of the war's progress resulted in an increase of American support for the war.

Ⓒ News with graphic images and interviews with frustrated soldiers resulted in a decrease of American public support for the war.

Ⓓ Although Walter Cronkite, a trusted television news anchor, supported the U.S. staying in the war, Americans started to decide it was not a good idea to stay in Vietnam.

20. Which social activist helped start a union for workers' rights in 1962 called the *National Farm Workers Association* (NFWA)?

Ⓐ Cesar Chavez

Ⓑ Felix Longoria

Ⓒ Hector P. Garcia

Ⓓ Martin Luther King, Jr.

Use the excerpt and your knowledge of social studies to answer the following question:

Excerpt from *The Black Experience in America* by Norman Coombs, 1972:

"In November [of 1963], Congressional debate on the Civil Rights Bill was still continuing, but the President had now made the passage of the Civil Rights Bill one of the most urgent goals of his Administration. But on the 22nd of November, John F. Kennedy was gunned down in the Presidential limousine in Dallas, Texas. The nation and the world were struck dumb with disbelief. Even those who had disliked his politics were horrified at the assassination of a President in a democratic state. His supporters felt that they had lost a friend as well as a leader...

The sense of shock caused despair and gloom. The fact that his successor, Lyndon B. Johnson, was a Southerner led most civil rights supporters to feel that there would be a reversal of federal policies on the racial question. However, Johnson immediately tried to reassure the nation that his intention was to carry on with the unfinished business of the Kennedy era."

21. Based on this excerpt and your knowledge of social studies, what could be predicted would happen next in history?

Ⓐ President Johnson did sign a Civil Rights Act, but not until 1967.

Ⓑ Congress passed a Civil Rights Act in 1964, and President Johnson signed it.

Ⓒ Congress passed a Civil Rights Act in 1964, but President Johnson did not sign it.

Ⓓ Without the leadership of President Kennedy, congress did not pass a Civil Rights Act until the 1970s.

Use the chart and your knowledge of social studies to answer the following question:

Participants	Date	Agreements Made
Israeli Prime Minister Menachem Begin (signer) to Egypt	1979	Israel agreed to return the Sinai
Egyptian President Anwar el-Sadat (signer)		Egypt and Israel agreed to work on Palestinian independence steps for the West Bank and Gaza
U.S. President Jimmy Carter (Witness)		

22. What would be the BEST title for this chart?

Ⓐ Arab Spring Agreements

Ⓑ Camp David Accords

Ⓒ Palestine Liberation Organization Treaty

Ⓓ Peace through Strength Plans

Use the excerpt and your knowledge of social studies to answer the following question:

Excerpt from *The Black Experience in America* by Norman Coombs, 1972

"He held that, when the rights of blacks were violated, they should be willing to die in the struggle to secure them:

"If white America doesn't think the Afro-American, especially the upcoming generation, is capable of adopting the guerrilla tactics now being used by oppressed people elsewhere on this earth, she is making a drastic mistake. She is underestimating the force that can do her the most harm.

"A real honest effort to remove the just grievances of the 22 million Afro-Americans must be made immediately or in a short time it will be too late."

"The slogan 'Black Power' exploded from a public address system in Greenwood, Mississippi, in the summer of 1966..."

23. Which historical figure was MOST likely the speaker of the long quote in this excerpt (the one that starts "If white America...")?

Ⓐ James Meredith

Ⓑ Malcolm X

Ⓒ Martin Luther King, Jr.

Ⓓ William Clay

Use the list and your knowledge of social studies to answer the following question:

Jobs
Land
Political freedoms
Religious freedoms

24. What is the BEST explanation for what the items on this list all had in common during the late 1800s?

Ⓐ These were all promises of President Theodore Roosevelt's administration

Ⓑ These were all reasons why immigrants came to America in hopes of better lives

Ⓒ These were all reasons why settlers made a rush to California and other western states

Ⓓ These were all things offered by the government to Native Americans at that time period

Use the excerpt and your knowledge of social studies to answer the following question:
"The earnestness of the Americans in the situation was proclaimed to the world by the English and French, and General Pershing placed his name and that of his country and men high on the wall of fame by unselfishly offering to France at the most critical period the use of his entire force, to be disposed of and assigned wherever General Foch and his staff decided to use them. Within a few days thereafter the American troops which had been in training were marched in to relieve the stressed English and French."

25. The author of this excerpt is describing a turning point in which war?

Ⓐ War of 1812

Ⓑ Spanish-American War

Ⓒ World War I

Ⓓ World War II

26. Who headed the National Association for the Advancement of Colored People (NAACP) in 1910, founded and edited the NAACP's journal *The Crisis*, and wrote many "muckraking" articles for *The Crisis* about civil rights for African Americans?

Ⓐ W.E.B. DuBois

Ⓑ Matthew Gaines

Ⓒ Marcus Garvey

Ⓓ Booker T. Washington

27. Which reason or reasons BEST explain why the U.S. Office of War Information included famous stars such as Ethel Merman in their radio broadcasts in the 1940s?

Ⓐ To build morale, raise spirits, and help convince women they needed to stay home while men went to war

Ⓑ To build morale, raise spirits, and help convince women to apply for wartime work

Ⓒ To convince women to buy tickets to Broadway shows to support the U.S. economy during wartime

Ⓓ To convince women to buy movie tickets to support the U.S. economy during wartime

Use the excerpt and your knowledge of social studies to answer the following question:
"As you know, I will soon be visiting the People's Republic of China and the Soviet Union. I go there with no illusions. We have great differences with both powers. We shall continue to have great differences. But peace depends on the ability of great powers to live together on the same planet despite their differences."

28. Which president gave this speech, as he was about to become the first U.S. President to visit the communist People's Republic of China?

Ⓐ President John F. Kennedy

Ⓑ President Lyndon B. Johnson

Ⓒ President Richard M. Nixon

Ⓓ President Gerald R. Ford

29. What event in April 1975 meant that the Vietnam War was over and that South Vietnam would surrender to the communists, leading to the eventual reunification of the country under communist rule?

Ⓐ Fall of Saigon

Ⓑ Ho Chi Minh's death

Ⓒ My Lai Massacre

Ⓓ Tet Offensive

30. "Old enough to fight, old enough to vote" became a slogan for a youth voting rights movement after the World War II military draft age was lowered to 18, while 21 remained the minimum voting age. The Vietnam War draft brought more urgency to the youth voting rights movement and resulted in which amendment to lower the voting age to 18?

Ⓐ 24th Amendment

Ⓑ 25th Amendment

Ⓒ 26th Amendment

Ⓓ 27th Amendment

Use the list and your knowledge of social studies to answer the following question:
    Poor agricultural practices
    Years of drought
    Lack of ground cover to hold soil in place
    High winds on the plains

31. What would be the BEST title to summarize this list?

Ⓐ Causes of the 1935 Dust Bowl

Ⓑ Effects of the 1935 Dust Bowl

Ⓒ Issues for the 1970s Era Rust Belt

Ⓓ Issues for the 1970s Era Sun Belt

Use the excerpt and your knowledge of social studies to answer the following question:
    Excerpt from <u>Crossing the Plains, Days of '57</u> by William Audley Maxwell, 1915
    "We forded the Platte at a point something like one hundred and fifty miles westward from its confluence with the Missouri. There was no road leading into the river, nor any evidence of its having been crossed by any one at that place. We were informed that the bottom was of quicksand, and fording, therefore, dangerous. We tested it, by riding horses across. Contrary to our expectations, the bottom was found to be a surface of smooth sand, packed hard enough to bear up the wagons, when the movement was quick and continuous. A cut was made in the bank, to form a runway for passage of the wagons to the water's edge; and the whole train crossed the stream safely, with no further mishap than the wetting of a driver and the dipping of a wagon into a place deep enough to let water into the box. Fording the Platte consumed one entire day. We camped that night on the north shore."

32. Which statement BEST summarizes the main idea of the above paragraph describing geographic factors for settlers headed to the Great Plains?

Ⓐ Fording the Platte River in stage coach wagons was dangerous because wagons often got caught in quicksand

Ⓑ Fording the Platte River was believed to be dangerous, but it turned out to be quick and easy for stage coach wagons

Ⓒ Fording the Platte River was thought to be dangerous, but it turned out to be mostly time-consuming and a little inconvenient

Ⓓ After fording the Platte River, stage coach wagons could continue driving west or could stop and camp for a night by the shore of the river

Use the chart and your knowledge of social studies to answer the following question:

U.S. Census Data

(All population figures are per 200,000 square miles of land area)

Date:	Northeastern U.S. Rural Areas	Northeastern U.S. Urban Areas
1890	Population average of around 7.5 million	Population average of around 12.5 million
1930	Population average of around 11 million	Population average of around 30 million

33. Which conclusion is MOST likely true based on this U.S. Census Data chart?

Ⓐ Rural to urban migration was a probable trend between the years 1890 and 1930.

Ⓑ Urban to rural migration was a probable pattern between the years 1890 and 1930.

Ⓒ Urban areas grew in population numbers but rural areas had a decreased population between 1890 and 1930.

Ⓓ Rural areas grew in population numbers but urban areas had a decreased population between 1890 and 1930.

Use the timeline and your knowledge of social studies to answer the following question:

1962 - The book "Silent Spring," by Rachel Carson, was published and soon became a bestseller. The book exposed the negative effects of pesticides on the environment in the U.S.

1969 - President Nixon set up a Cabinet-level "Environmental Quality Council" as well as a "Citizens' Advisory Committee on Environmental Quality."

1970 - In February, President Nixon announced stronger federal programs to deal with water and air pollution.

1970 - In April that year, the first Earth Day was celebrated in the U.S. by about 20 million Americans.

34. Based on this timeline, which event MOST likely took place in December of 1970?

Ⓐ Future Vice President Al Gore gave a report on global warming to his fellow college students

Ⓑ Vietnam War protests overshadowed the public concern for a healthy environment and the issue faded away for a while

Ⓒ President Nixon oversaw the establishment of the National Park System, setting aside lands for protection and public recreation

Ⓓ President Nixon oversaw the establishment of the Environmental Protection Agency to consolidate pollution control and environmental protection

35. "Sustainable development" is defined as development that meets the needs of the present while still making possible the ability of future generations to meet their needs. It takes into account environmental impacts and tries to minimize damage to the environment. Which reason BEST describes why there is a need for sustainable development?

Ⓐ The environment will always evolve to adapt to the needs of future generations

Ⓑ Future generations will not have as many scientists because education is deteriorating

Ⓒ Population growth has stabilized, but there are still future stresses on the environment such as global warming

Ⓓ The continued forecasted population growth can damage the environment with greater stresses on oceans, food supplies, and land

36. In the 1960s, "Beat Generation" member Allen Ginsberg worked with psychologist Timothy Leary to promote more widespread use of the drug LSD. What was an impact of this on American society?

Ⓐ More widespread use made the drug LSD more popular and it became a legal drug.

Ⓑ LSD was a legal drug until the 1980s "War on Drugs" made it an illegal substance.

Ⓒ Politicians were some people who experimented with LSD and it made them more open-minded about political issues.

Ⓓ While some people may have felt that LSD was psychologically helpful, many people experienced bad effects such as fear or psychosis from the drug, and the drug was and is still illegal.

Use the excerpt and your knowledge of social studies to answer the following question:
In this excerpt from *The Black Experience in America* (1972), author Norman Coombs describes the 1920s Harlem Renaissance:
"Students, peasants, artists, businessmen, professional men, poets, musicians, and workers; all came to Harlem...Langston Hughes, in describing his first entrance into Harlem from the 135th Street subway exit, said that he felt vitality and hope throbbing in the air. In Black Manhattan, James Weldon Johnson said that Harlem was not a slum or a fringe. Rather, he insisted that it was one of the "most beautiful and healthful sections of the city."

37. Based on the excerpt, what was one probable impact of the Harlem Renaissance for African-American society?

 Ⓐ It made African Americans feel like they were relegated to a ghetto culture

 Ⓑ It gave African Americans a new sense of pride and confidence in their culture

 Ⓒ The Harlem Renaissance made black people feel like they should only live in the Harlem area of Manhattan and not in any other cities

 Ⓓ The Harlem Renaissance was helpful for black artists, musicians, and writers, but not for businessmen or other professional black people

Use the list and your knowledge of social studies to answer the following question:
- Islamic rap groups in England and France
- A Basque group in Spain called Negu Gorriak that incorporates U.S. hip-hop
- Musicians in New Zealand who combine rap, soul and reggae with traditional Maori music

38. What is the BEST generalization that could be made based on this list?

 Ⓐ American culture can spread globally through entertainment such as rap and hip-hop music, but that same culture sometimes gets reconstituted into new forms in other countries

 Ⓑ Rap and hip-hop music have spread from the U.S. to Spain, England, France, and New Zealand, but not to any other countries

 Ⓒ Rap and hip-hop music are examples of ways that Hollywood influences culture in other countries

 Ⓓ Rap and hip-hop music arose originally in other countries before becoming popular in the U.S.

39. Which choice BEST shows the contributions of Italian-American women to U.S. culture in the field of politics?

 Ⓐ Sylvia Scaramelli helped co-found a college in New Jersey in 1942; Suzette Charles (born Suzette De Gaetano) was the first Italian American to win the Miss America title

 Ⓑ The first woman to run for Vice President of the United States was Geraldine Ferraro in 1984; the first woman elected governor in her own right was Ella T. Grasso of Connecticut in 1975

 Ⓒ Jerre Mangione wrote about the history of Italian Americans; Dr. Rosemarie Truglio studied the effects of television on children and teenagers

 Ⓓ Sonia Sotomayor is a current female Supreme Court Justice; Don DeLillo is an Italian-American author

40. In which movement were members of the Quaker religious group NOT very active?

Ⓐ Abolitionist movement

Ⓑ McCarthyism movement

Ⓒ Pacifist and peace activist movements

Ⓓ Women's rights movement

41. Which First Lady was honorary vice chair of the Red Cross and led blood donation and fundraising drives during a war?

Ⓐ Edith Bolling Galt Wilson

Ⓑ Eleanor Roosevelt

Ⓒ Lady Bird Johnson

Ⓓ Pat Nixon

42. More than one elementary school in Texas is named after Roy Benavidez, a Mexican American born in Texas, and he was buried with full military honors at Fort Sam Houston National Cemetery. Why?

Ⓐ He was the first Mexican American to serve in the army and become a state senator in Texas

Ⓑ He was the first Mexican American to become a high-ranking officer in the army in the 1950s

Ⓒ He won a Congressional Medal of Honor for his brave military service during the Korean War

Ⓓ He won a Congressional Medal of Honor and a Purple Heart for his brave military service and actions in the Vietnam War

43. When the FBI examined homes of Japanese Americans without warrants during World War II, which constitutional right of those Japanese Americans was violated?

Ⓐ Right to reasonable bail

Ⓑ Freedom of the press

Ⓒ Freedom from unreasonable searches and seizures

Ⓓ Right to a speedy and public trial

44. How did all Native Americans achieve U.S. citizenship?

(A) By marrying white American citizens

(B) By serving in American military units

(C) By studying for and passing a citizenship test

(D) Through passage of the American Indian Citizenship Act of 1924

Use the excerpt and your knowledge of social studies to answer the following question:
Excerpt from *Integration of the Armed Forces, 1940-1965*, by Morris J. MacGregor, Jr.

"The laws of 1866 and 1869 that guaranteed the existence of four black Regular Army regiments also institutionalized segregation, granting federal recognition to a system racially separate and theoretically equal in treatment and opportunity a generation before the Supreme Court sanctioned such a distinction in *Plessy* v. *Ferguson*."

45. Which option BEST describes what was sanctioned by the Supreme Court in the *Plessy v. Ferguson* case of 1896?

(A) Segregation, or the idea of separate but equal treatment for African Americans

(B) Integration and equal treatment for African Americans

(C) Army regiments that had a majority of black servicemen

(D) Army regiments that had only black servicemen

46. In the 1954 *Hernandez v. Texas* case, the Supreme Court decided that white and Hispanic could be considered different "classes" because of the way Hispanics had been unfairly treated in Texas. What was a MAIN effect of this decision?

(A) Hispanics accused of crimes still faced juries composed only of white Americans

(B) African Americans also started to be considered as a different class, instead of as a different race

(C) Hispanics were now an identifiable minority group and their segregation could be prohibited under the *Brown* decision of 1954

(D) Civil rights activists used the different class concept as their legal strategy for the next several decades, and the 14th Amendment was now applied to Hispanics as well as to African Americans

47. If a high school student wanted to wear an armband to protest the U.S. military presence in Afghanistan, which Supreme Court decision could the student cite as allowing him or her to wear that armband into school (as long as the student did not disrupt classes)?

(A) *Hazelwood School District v. Kuhlmeier*, 1988

(B) *Bethel School District No. 403 v. Fraser*, 1986

(C) *Tinker v. Des Moines*, 1969

(D) *Doremus v. Board of Education of Borough of Hawthorne*, 1952

48. In 1937, President Franklin D. Roosevelt was accused by opponents of trying to "pack the court," and his plan for courts was defeated by the U.S. Senate. What was Roosevelt's plan for the judicial branch at that time?

(A) Roosevelt wanted only Democrats to be appointed to federal district courts

(B) Roosevelt wanted only Democrats to be appointed as Supreme Court justices

(C) Roosevelt wanted to raise the total number of Supreme Court justices from nine to 15

(D) Roosevelt wanted to raise the total number of federal district court judges from 94 to 100

49. Which choice below BEST shows an example of how one can "lobby" a congressperson?

(A) Voting for your congressperson during an election campaign

(B) Voting for your congressperson's opponent during an election

(C) Reading the email newsletters your congressperson sends to supporters

(D) Writing a letter to your congressperson about an issue that is important to you

Question 50 pertains to the following excerpt from *The Black Experience in America*, author Norman Coombs describes a 1960s sit-in:

> "In a matter of weeks, student sit-ins were occurring at segregated lunch counters all across the South. College and high school students by the thousands joined the Civil Rights Movement. These students felt the need to form their own organization to mobilize and facilitate the spontaneous demonstrations which were springing up everywhere."

50. Student "sit-ins" are BEST described as which kind of way to participate in the democratic process?

Ⓐ Displaying Black Power to incite fear

Ⓑ Litigating

Ⓒ Lobbying

Ⓓ Non-violent protesting

51. In the PATRIOT Act first passed after September 11, 2001, the government could monitor religious and political institutions without suspecting criminal activity just in case it might assist a terror investigation. Which phrase BEST describes a constitutional right violated by such actions?

Ⓐ Right to legal representation

Ⓑ Right to a speedy and public trial

Ⓒ Right against involuntary servitude

Ⓓ Freedom of association or assembly

Use the excerpt and your knowledge of social studies to answer the following question:
Alexis de Tocqueville, in Democracy in America, wrote in 1840 about America
"The nearer the citizens are drawn to the common level of an equal and similar condition, the less prone does each man become to place implicit faith in a certain man or a certain class of men. But his readiness to believe the multitude increases, and opinion is more than ever mistress of the world. Not only is common opinion the only guide which private judgment retains amongst a democratic people, but amongst such a people it possesses a power infinitely beyond what it has elsewhere."

52. Which American traits was Alexis de Tocqueville describing in this excerpt?

Ⓐ Egalitarianism and populism

Ⓑ Individualism and liberty

Ⓒ Laissez-faire politics and individualism

Ⓓ Populism and liberty

53. The Sherman Antitrust Act of 1890 was the first federal law attempting to limit what kind of businesses?

Ⓐ Businesses that had monopolies or cartels

Ⓑ Businesses owned by foreigners

Ⓒ Companies that used child laborers

Ⓓ Companies that had lost the trust of their customers

54. What was an economic effect of the 1862 Homestead Act?

Ⓐ Agriculture became the top business in the U.S.

Ⓑ The Homestead Act led to the formation of a "Farmers for the Economy" political group

Ⓒ Pioneers moved westward, built towns and schools, and created new states from former territories

Ⓓ The Act did not give enough incentives for people to move west, so the frontier did not get settled until much later in the 1800s

55. What was an economic effect of the Spanish-American War that could MOST likely be considered a positive economic benefit for the U.S.?

Ⓐ Acquisition of island territories that could provide new markets

Ⓑ Chance to invest money in Spain and other foreign countries

Ⓒ Cost of rebuilding ships that had been damaged in the war

Ⓓ Cost of sending aid to poor people in Cuba

56. In war times, a government typically has three main ways to raise money to finance a war: borrowing from the public, printing money, and a third way. During World War I, the U.S. government did not want to directly print money, as that might have driven down the gold standard. What was the third way to raise money for the war that was used in 1917?

Ⓐ Borrowing money from foreign governments

Ⓑ Cutting domestic government programs

Ⓒ Raising taxes, in the form of a War Revenue Act

Ⓓ Selling war bonds to the public

57. Speculation, which sometimes includes risky business transactions for a possible quick profit, was common regarding housing prices around 2003-2007, helping cause the current economic recession. What is one similarity between this fact and a cause of the 1929-1930s Great Depression?

Ⓐ Housing prices became too high in the 1930s, helping cause the Great Depression

Ⓑ Speculation on housing prices in the 1920s helped cause the Great Depression

Ⓒ Speculation in the 1920s stock market helped cause the Great Depression

Ⓓ A 1920s recession led to the Great Depression

58. World trade declined by 66 percent from 1929 to 1934, helping cause the Great Depression of 1929-1939. What form of U.S. "protectionism" helped cause the decline in world trade?

Ⓐ Bank failures across the U.S.

Ⓑ The monetary policy of the Federal Reserve System

Ⓒ The lowering of U.S. tariffs on imported goods

Ⓓ The raising of U.S. tariffs on imported goods

Use the graph and your knowledge of social studies to answer the following question:

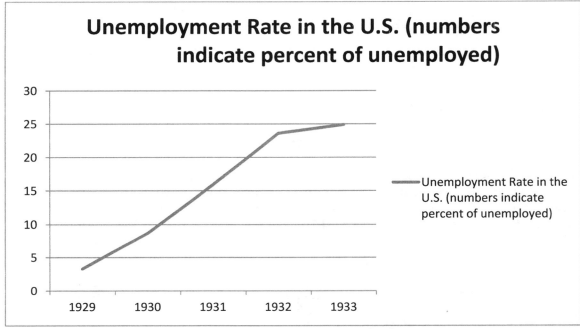

Statistics from the U.S. Bureau of Labor

59. What is one conclusion that can be made based on this chart?

Ⓐ High U.S. unemployment starting in 1929 helped cause the Great Depression

Ⓑ U.S. unemployment was higher in the early 1930s than unemployment in other countries

Ⓒ High U.S. unemployment showed a small decrease and then held steady in the early 1930s

Ⓓ The Great Depression caused a steep increase in the rate of unemployment in the U.S.

60. From 1929-1939, the Mexican population in the U.S. dropped by 40 percent. What was a main cause of this drop?

Ⓐ The Great Depression and lack of jobs led Mexican Americans to voluntarily leave the U.S.

Ⓑ The Great Depression led to mass deportations of Mexican Americans by the U.S. government

Ⓒ Many Mexican Americans had served in World War I and did not want to fight in future wars for the U.S.

Ⓓ Mexican Americans were tiring of the racism and discrimination in the U.S. and were voluntarily leaving the U.S.

Use the list and your knowledge of social studies to answer the following question:
- During World War II, the U.S. government put out the following list of information (paraphrased below) on why people should use less sugar in their kitchens:
- Soldiers need sugar, and overall military needs for sugar are high.
- The ships that usually bring sugar into the U.S. are being used to bring supplies to battle fronts.
- There are currently not enough workers at sugar refineries and shipping ports due to the need for military service people.
- In summary, do not apply for more sugar than you really need!

61. What was the name and reason for this government program?

Ⓐ Food Safety Act, to ensure that food supplies were safe during the war

Ⓑ G.I. Bill, to ensure that servicemen got enough food and other supplies

Ⓒ New Deal, to ensure that poorer families would get enough food supplies during the war

Ⓓ Rationing, because important supplies, including food, were scarce and in high demand during the war

Use the list and your knowledge of social studies to answer the following question:
- U.S. shipbuilding industry
- Los Alamos nuclear facility
- All-American Girls Professional Baseball League
- Washington D.C. government office jobs

62. Which choice BEST describes what the items on the above list have in common?

Ⓐ These were areas where women could find employment in non-traditional ways because of manpower shortage during World War I

Ⓑ These were areas where women could find employment in non-traditional ways because of manpower shortage during World War II

Ⓒ These were all organizations that received federal government funding in the 1930s

Ⓓ These were all organizations the received federal government funding in the 1940s

Use the excerpt and your knowledge of social studies to answer the following question:
In this excerpt from *The Black Experience in America*, author Norman Coombs describes 1941 negotiations between civil rights activist A. Philip Randolph, who was planning a March on Washington by African Americans, and President Franklin D. Roosevelt:

"Finally, Roosevelt contacted Randolph and offered to issue an executive order barring discrimination in defense industries and promised to put "teeth" in the order, provided Randolph call off the march. When Randolph became convinced that Roosevelt's intentions were sincere, he complied.

Roosevelt fulfilled his promise by issuing Executive Order 8802, which condemned discrimination on the grounds of race, color, or creed. Then, he established the Fair Employment Practices Commission and assigned to it the responsibility for enforcing the order."

63. What conclusion can BEST be made based on this excerpt?

Ⓐ Jobs for African Americans increased during World War II because of manpower needs and because of an anti-discrimination order from the president

Ⓑ Jobs for African Americans increased during World War II because of manpower needs alone, and the anti-discrimination order was probably not really needed

Ⓒ A. Philip Randolph was just bluffing about planning a March on Washington

Ⓓ President Franklin D. Roosevelt was not really worried about African Americans marching on Washington, but he gave in to Randolph's request for an Executive Order anyway

Use the "Cause and Effects" chart and your knowledge of social studies to answer the following question:

Cause: An important bill is passed in both Congress and the Senate and signed by President Franklin D. Roosevelt in 1944.

↓

Effect: Men with only high school educations could now go to college.

↓

Effect: Some of those men became doctors, lawyers, engineers, or joined other middle class professions.

↓

Effect: The middle class jobs and loans from the same bill allow men to buy houses.

↓

Effect: Entire suburbs are built with new homes for newly middle class families.

64. Complete this "Cause and Effects" chart by filling in a missing piece of information for "Cause." What was the name of the bill passed in 1944?

Ⓐ Executive Order 9981

Ⓑ G.I. Bill

Ⓒ Smith Act of 1944

Ⓓ Taft-Hartley Act

65. The 1950s included growing income and affluence, a larger middle class, and a baby boom. What other 1950s trend can BEST be considered an effect of those three factors?

Ⓐ Increased consumer spending and consumption

Ⓑ Military-industrial complex

Ⓒ Rock and roll music

Ⓓ The Cold War

66. The GATT (General Agreement on Tariffs and Trade) organization was started in 1947 by about 150 countries, including the U.S., to help regulate trade between them. What is the new name of the organization that GATT has now become, and is the U.S. still a member?

Ⓐ International Trade Administration (ITA); yes, the U.S. is still a member

Ⓑ International Trade Administration (ITA); no, the U.S. is no longer a member

Ⓒ World Trade Organization (WTO), yes, the U.S. is still a member

Ⓓ World Trade Organization (WTO); no, the U.S. is no longer a member

67. The first laptop computers were produced in the early 1980s and the cost to buy one was over $1,000. What are some reasons that laptop computers cost less today?

Ⓐ The government has set price controls on products such as laptop computers that would be used in businesses

Ⓑ In the free enterprise system, many companies now produce laptop computers and compete to sell them at lower costs

Ⓒ The earliest laptop computers had a sales tax added to their cost that has since been removed by government legislation

Ⓓ Laptop computers today can perform better and they have more functionality and memory than the earliest laptop computers had

68. What advantages does the 20ᵗʰ century invention of electric cars contribute to improving the standard of living in the U.S. (assuming that they are used)?

Ⓐ Electric cars go faster than gas-powered vehicles so they could improve efficiency, convenience, and productivity in the U.S.

Ⓑ Electric cars have better creature comforts in their interiors than gas-powered cars, increasing the standard of living for Americans using such cars

Ⓒ Electric cars take less time to recharge than gas-powered cars take to re-fuel, thereby improving U.S. efficiency, convenience, and productivity

Ⓓ Electric cars have no tailpipe emissions, helping the U.S. have less air pollution; they lessen the U.S.'s dependence on foreign oil; and they are cheaper to operate than gas-powered cars, helping Americans save money

Answers and Explanations

1. D: It gives the correct defining characteristic of the Roaring Twenties Era. The economy was strong with a great demand for new products, while culture in this era, also known as the "Jazz Age," became more experimental. A student might pick choice A, which defines the Cold War Era, if he or she focuses on the fact that it is also an era immediately following a World War. A student can rule out the other choices if they know how to correctly define the World War II and Great Depression Eras.

2. C: Jonathan Trumbull is the correct answer for which Founding Father was governor of Connecticut during and after the Revolutionary War. The other names are all of Founding Fathers, but none were governor of Connecticut. Rush, Witherspoon and Carroll all signed the Declaration of Independence; Carroll was a U.S. Senator for Maryland while Rush lived in Pennsylvania and Witherspoon in New Jersey.

3. A: It shows the student's knowledge of the importance of 1914 events as a turning point for the start of World War I in Europe: "World War I had started; Germany had invaded other Belgian cities and was going to invade Antwerp also." The other choices are incorrect because Italy, Russia, and England were not invading Belgium.

4. D: It lists true contributions by John Jay to early. Choice A is partly correct about the first Chief Justice, but Jay was a Minister to Spain, not to France. Choice B correctly places him in New York, but he did not sign the Declaration or become mayor of New York City. Choice C has Minister of Spain correct, but Jay did not serve in George Washington's army during the war.

5. D: Ella Baker was a civil rights leader but born in 1903. Rosa Parks was part of the 1960s civil rights movement. Sojourner Truth lived near the time of Ida B. Wells, but she had died by 1883. Ida B. Wells is the correct answer, and she was known as a journalist, muckraker, reform leader, and fighter against lynchings.

6. D: While the photo shows World War I airplane warfare over England, it also took place over other countries like Germany and France, so choice A is incorrect. Airplane warfare first took place after the invention of the airplane, so during the Civil War could not be a correct choice. The American allies and the German side went back and forth in terms of airplane technology superiority, so choice B is not correct. Choice D is the MOST likely answer choice. Airplanes had their first warfare use during WWI, at first just for taking spy photographs, but were also used later in the war for firing guns and dropping bombs. The photo illustrates the fact that airplanes were in use during WWI for firing guns and dropping bombs.

7. A: Sanford B. Dole was the President of the Republic of Hawaii, and he did argue for annexation of Hawaii by the United States. Students familiar with the time period should know that he was not the President of the United States or the President of the U.S. Senate. The excerpt may help them realize this fact. Also, Hawaii did not become a state officially until the 1950s, so choice B is incorrect.

8. B: The BEST summarizing title for the list is "How the Spanish-American War Helped the U.S. Become a World Power." President Theodore Roosevelt did help the U.S. become a world power, but that was after the events on the list (Spanish-American War events) because he was not president until 1901, after the war of 1898. Isolationism did give way to Imperialism in the 1890s, but it did not lead to or cause imperialism. The War of 1812 is an incorrect answer for students who know their historical dates and war events.

9. D: In point 14 of his 1918 speech Wilson was proposing a League of Nations which would eventually become the United Nations. If the student reads the excerpt carefully, and knows general history about the United Nations, the student will know that having the U.S. involved in such a league would be a contrast to Wilson's pre-War policy of neutrality. The other choices given make references to phrases found in the excerpt, but they are not statements that contrast with a policy of neutrality and are incorrect answer choices.

10. A: The 16th Amendment is the correct answer for which amendment dealt with collecting income taxes to help fund progressive government goals. While all the amendments listed were championed by Progressive Era reformers, and all were around the same time period, the other amendments listed dealt with voting issues or prohibition, not with income taxes.

11. D: It is correct for why the Battle of the Argonne Forest was difficult and important. The illustration gives a clue to the answer because it shows a deep trench (though it also shows a forest, so the student also needs general social studies knowledge). The battle was difficult because the Germans were so entrenched in this forest, having built deep trenches there; and important because it was one of the final battles of the war and helped break through Germany's western front. The deeply forested nature of the area mentioned in choice C was also a difficulty, but that choice is incorrect because it claims the Germans won that battle when they did not. Some German soldiers were taken as prisoners of war during the battle, and there may have been some Allied prisoners, but that was not the purpose of the battle. There was air support provided to the Allies in that battle, so choice A is incorrect.

12. C: It is the BEST and only definition of the initiative process: It allowed citizens to introduce legislation proposals at a local or state level by gathering petitions, and proposals would then be addressed by lawmakers or placed on ballots for a vote. The other answer choices give definitions of "referendum" (choice A), "recall" (choice B), and also describe simply visiting a state legislature to give testimony about an issue (choice D), none of which define the "initiative" process.

13. B: "Nativism," a philosophy of the time period that native-born white Americans were superior to foreign born Americans, helped cause the Emergency Quota Act that limited immigrants in 1921. The other options were all social issues of the same time period, but not the main cause for limiting immigration. The Harlem Renaissance and Women's Suffrage Movement did not have such qualms with immigrants. Prohibition was partly caused by anti-immigrant sentiment such as against Germans after WWI, but Prohibition did not cause the Quota Act as much as Nativism.

14. C: It would BEST go next in the timeline's factual sequence of events because the other choices are not factually correct: thousands of Japanese-American men, women and children are relocated to internment camps. They were not forced to leave the U.S., and they were not forced to move from west coast to east coast (many internment camps were on the west coast). Japanese-American men did eventually start to be drafted for military service during World War II, and many did fight in that war for the U.S.

- 142 -

15. D: It is the correct answer for this particular group of children, although choices A and B might be good guesses. There were German youth who wanted to avoid serving in Nazi armies, but they did not go into hiding in as great numbers as did Jewish youth trying to escape the Holocaust. There were children who awaited fake passports, but mostly to escape to the U.S. or other safe countries, as Israel was not founded until after World War II. The correct answer is that "They were Jewish and had to be hidden from Nazis in order to survive the Holocaust, the attempted extermination of the Jewish population by Nazi Germany."

16. D: The Tuskegee Airmen was another name for the 332nd Fighter Group. The African-American men in the photo give the clue that it was the Tuskegee Airmen and not the Flying Tigers, who were Chinese American. The Tuskegee Airmen were an African-American group of fighter pilots in WWII, which should be general social studies knowledge at this grade level. Red Barons were in WWI, and Top Guns are navy pilots, nicknamed in a later time period than WWII.

17. A: NATO formed for the purpose of defending Europe from possible encroachment by communist Soviet Union armies which had invaded and were controlling some central and eastern European countries after WWII. Choice B and C may have eventually become other purposes for NATO in later years, but were not the original reasons for the formation of NATO. Choice D is incorrect because Germany did not immediately reunite after the war.

18. D: The Vietnam War was fought by the U.S. in Vietnam because of the Domino Theory. China was the "first domino" in the theory, in that it became a communist nation before other Asian countries, but the U.S. did not fight a war there. The U.S. has also had shaky relations with Burma more recently, but did not fight a war there or in Thailand.

19. C: It is the correct result from the increased media coverage and availability. News with graphic images and interviews with frustrated soldiers resulted in a decrease of American public support for the war. It did not result in increased American support or in more men registering for the draft. The choice about Walter Cronkite could be a good guess, except that in 1970 Cronkite declared the war a "bloody stalemate," thus echoing and influencing the opinions of a majority of Americans about the Vietnam War.

20. A: Cesar Chavez, along with Dolores Huerta and Gilbert Padilla, helped start the NFWA in 1962. Students who know a little about Chavez and his lifelong activism for Hispanic migrant workers should be able to choose the correct answer. A student might incorrectly pick Hector P. Garcia or Felix Longoria for being others from the Mexican American civil rights movements (Garcia a doctor, and Longoria a WWII soldier). Or a student might pick Martin Luther King, Jr. because he also helped workers form unions, although not as much for farmers as for urban city workers.

21. B: The excerpt states that Johnson did want to carry on Kennedy's agenda and legacy, and that included in the field of Civil Rights, despite Johnson originally being a southerner. So the correct answer is B, Congress passed a Civil Rights Act in 1964 and President Johnson signed it. Students reading the excerpt carefully and having a good general knowledge of civil rights history should be able to make that correct prediction.

22. B: The Camp David Accords is the correct name for this historical event which included the 1979 leaders of Egypt and Israel making agreements with both the help and witnessing of U.S. President Jimmy Carter. The Arab Spring is a more current event (2010-2011), and Peace through Strength was a Reagan-era philosophy. Palestinians are mentioned in the Camp David Accords, so choice C could be a good guess, but general social studies knowledge of the Middle East should help students remember that the PLO is Yasser Arafat's organization.

23. B: Malcolm X is the correct speaker of the excerpt's long quotation, as he is the only one on the list from the Black Power movement. James Sherman did a Freedom March and was murdered, which inspired some Black Power rallies, but he himself was not the advocate of a less peaceful movement. Martin Luther King, Jr. was the main advocate of nonviolent social change, so he would not have spoken the quote about "guerrilla tactics." William Clay was a representative and leader of the Black Caucus in Congress, not a revolutionary figure.

24. B: Jobs, land, and religious and political freedoms were all reasons why immigrants imagined that they would have better lives by coming to America in the late 1800s. Theodore Roosevelt was not president until 1901. Native Americans were not promised all of these things during that time period, or at least that would not be the BEST answer. Settlers did rush to California and the west for land, but not for the other items on that list, and gold is not on the list, which makes that choice a poor answer option.

25. C: The clue in the excerpt about American troops helping the stressed French and British troops should let the student know that the excerpt refers to World War I or World War II. If they read closely enough to see General Pershing's involvement, then they should know from general social studies knowledge at this grade level that Pershing was the commander of American Expeditionary Forces during World War I, and therefore C is the correct answer.

26. A: W.E.B. DuBois was a famous African American muckraking journalist for the NAACP's magazine in the early 1900s. Booker T. Washington was a contemporary of DuBois, but not a muckraking journalist. Gaines was a former slave who became a Texas State Senator, but Gaines died in 1900 and therefore could not be the correct answer. Marcus Garvey had a writing career advocating civil rights, but in a newspaper he started called *The Negro World*.

27. B: Students who know about the U.S. Office of War Information should know that the purpose was to get out messages that would build morale and raise spirits. They also tried to recruit women for wartime work during WWII. They sometimes used famous stars such as Ethel Merman to further appeal to women. Their purpose was not to sell Broadway or movie tickets, nor was it to encourage women to stay at home.

28. C: The speech is from President Richard M. Nixon, who was about to become, in 1972, the first U.S. president to visit the People's Republic of China. The other presidents listed are good guesses as they are from similar time periods and might have made similar speeches about China and the Soviet Union, but they are incorrect choices.

29. A: The Fall of Saigon happened in April 1975 and marked the end of the Vietnam War and the beginning of Vietnam's reunification under communist rule. A student might pick one of the other events because they were all events that did happen in the course of the

Vietnam War, but they happened on earlier dates, not in April 1975, and were not the final event that marked the end of the war or South Vietnam's surrender.

30. C: The 26th Amendment is the youth voting rights amendment allowing 18-year-olds to vote, signed by President Nixon. The Vietnam War gave more urgency to the "old enough to fight, old enough to vote" slogan. The other amendment choices are in similar time frames and close enough to the 26th Amendment to possibly confuse a student who has not fully studied some of the more important amendments such as the 26th.

31. A: It is the BEST title for the list, The Causes of the 1935 Dust Bowl. The lack of ground cover was a cause of the Dust Bowl, but could also be considered a possible effect of dust storms also. But that is the only item on the list that would also be an effect of the Dust Bowl. The Sun Belt also had some years of drought, but the other items would not fit for Sun Belt as much, or for the Rust Belt except for possibly poor agricultural practices.

32. C: It is the BEST summary of the paragraph's main idea for settlers headed to the Great Plains in stage coach wagons: Fording the Platte River was thought to be dangerous, but turned out to mostly be time-consuming and a little inconvenient: time consuming because it "consumed" a whole day and inconvenient in that drivers and wagon boxes got wet. Choice A is incorrect because the wagon in the paragraph did not get caught in quicksand. Choice B is incorrect because it was not a quick and easy fording (it consumed a whole day). Choice D is a correct and true statement, but it has to do with a detail of the trip after the river crossing, and does not deal with the paragraph's main idea of describing the river crossing.

33. A: The most likely conclusion based on the U.S. Census data chart is that rural to urban migration was a probable trend between the years 1890 and 1930. Both rural and urban areas grew in population numbers, making choices C and D incorrect, but urban areas grew by a much larger margin, meaning that there was probably migration from rural areas in addition to general population growth as a factor for the different numbers. Choice B is incorrect because urban to rural migration numbers are not shown on the chart.

34. D: Choice A is incorrect because Al Gore was not yet speaking on global warming issues during that time period. Choice B does not make sense in the context of the timeline because all the other events listed deal with environmental issues. Choice C confuses the establishment of the National Park System with the EPA. The park system was established earlier by Theodore Roosevelt, which should be part of the student's general social studies knowledge. Choice D is correct: Nixon established the EPA in December 1970.

35. D: It is the best reason why sustainable development is needed: The continued, forecasted population growth can damage the environment with greater stresses on oceans, food supplies, and land. Even though global warming (mentioned in choice C) is another reason why sustainable development is needed, the statement in choice C that population growth has stabilized is false. Fertility rates have fallen in some areas, but the world population will continue to expand for many years before possibly stabilizing. Choices A and B are not completely true statements and not good reasons for sustainable development.

36. D: A student picking answer D shows an understanding of a negative impact of the Beat Generation promoting the drug LSD: While some people may have felt that LSD was psychologically helpful, many people experienced bad effects such as fear or psychosis from the drug, and the drug was and still is illegal. The drug has been illegal since 1966, so choices A and B are incorrect. Choice C is also incorrect in that politicians were not the main people influenced by the Beat Generation to experiment with the drug.

37. B: Reading the excerpt and the proud quotes in it about Harlem should lead students to the correct answer about the impact of the Harlem Renaissance on African-American society in the 1920s: it gave African Americans a new sense of pride and confidence in their culture. It did not make them feel relegated to a "ghetto," as they chose to live in Harlem and made it a nice place to live. But blacks also lived in other cities, making choice C incorrect. Choice D is incorrect because the first part of the excerpt describes all kinds of people coming to participate in the Harlem Renaissance, not just artists, musicians, and writers, as might be popularly thought to be true.

38. A: It is the right choice for a generalization based on the bulleted list: American culture can spread globally through entertainment such as rap and hip-hop music, but that same culture sometimes gets reconstituted into new forms in other countries. Choice B is incorrect because rap and hip-hop have spread from the U.S. to other countries also. Hollywood was not the main medium for spreading rap and hip-hop, since they are forms of music and not films, making choice C incorrect. Choice D is incorrect because rap and hip-hop mostly originated in the U.S.

39. B: It best shows contributions of Italian-American women in the field of politics: The first woman to run for U.S. Vice President was Geraldine Ferraro in 1984, and the first woman elected governor in her own right was Ella T. Grasso of Connecticut in 1975. The other choices show Italian-American women (or in one case a Latina woman, Sonia Sotomayor) making contributions in other fields that are not as political (education, Miss America, etc.). Some of the names listed are actually Italian-American men: Don DeLillo and Jerre Mangione.

40. B: Students with general social studies knowledge at this grade level will have heard of the Quaker religious group, who were active in the Abolitionist movement, women's rights movement, and pacifist/peace movements throughout U.S. history, because all those movements agree with their religious views on equality and peace. The correct answer of B, the McCarthyism movement, is therefore an example of one movement that Quakers were NOT as involved in. In fact, Edward R. Murrow, one of the biggest opponents of McCarthy's "Un-American Activities Committee," was raised as a Quaker.

41. B: Eleanor Roosevelt was the First Lady who was also an honorary chair of the Red Cross. However, all of the First Ladies listed were First Ladies during war times, so they could be good guesses. But a student who knows the particular contributions of Eleanor Roosevelt to American politics and society should know the correct answer.

42. D: It best explains the fame and military burial honors for Mexican-American Roy Benavidez: He won a Congressional Medal of Honor and a Purple Heart for his brave military service and actions in the Vietnam War. He did serve in the Korean War briefly, but did not win his awards for that service. Choices A and B are false statements.

43. C: The freedom from unreasonable search and seizure was the constitutional right violated by the FBI when they searched the homes of Japanese Americans without search warrants during World War II. The other rights may have been violated in other ways by

- 146 -

the government at the same time (also against Japanese Americans), but not in this particular given example. A student that understands the Constitution will answer correctly.

44. D: All Native Americans were granted U.S. citizenship by the American Indian Citizenship Act of 1924. Having to take a citizenship test sounds correct, as many immigrants do that today, but it is not the correct answer. It is correct that some Native Americans achieved citizenship by marrying white citizens or by serving in the U.S. military, but not all Native Americans became citizens until passage of the act in 1924.

45. A: A student reading the excerpt closely and knowing their general social studies history about *Plessy v. Ferguson* will choose the correct answer for what it decreed: segregation, or the idea of separate but equal treatment, for African Americans. A student might be fooled by the book title's "integration" mention to choose answer B. Or they may focus on the mention of black servicemen in the excerpt and incorrectly choose answers C or D. Choice D could describe an effect of *Plessy v. Ferguson*, but not the official thing being sanctioned. Choice A describes the sanction AND the effect of *Plessy v. Ferguson*.

46. D: Civil rights activists used the different "class," or "other white," concept as their legal strategy for the next several decades, and the 14th Amendment was now applied to Hispanics as well as to African Americans. This was the main effect of the *Hernandez v. Texas* decision. It did not have the effect described in choice C, as that happened in a 1970s Supreme Court case. Choice A was the problem being addressed in the Hernandez case, not an effect. And choice B has to do with African Americans, not Hispanics.

47. C: In 1969, *Tinker v. Des Moines* gave students the right to maintain their First Amendment right of free speech; in that case, wearing an armband to protest the Vietnam War, even inside of school buildings (as long as classes were not disrupted). The other cases also involve school districts and education, but were for different specific issues than this one. Although the Bethel and Kuhlmeier cases also touched on the First Amendment, in those cases it was in relation to school assemblies and school newspapers, not school attire.

48. C: President Roosevelt's plan for the judicial branch in 1937 was to raise the total number of Supreme Court justices from 9 to 15. His plan was defeated by the U.S. Senate. The other answer choices sound like plausible ways that one might try to "pack the courts," but they are not correct answers for that time period, which students with a general history knowledge at this grade level should know.

49. D: Writing a letter to your congressperson about an issue that is important to you is the BEST example of how to "lobby" a congressperson. (Visiting, calling, or emailing are other lobbying methods.) Just reading the congressperson's email might be a first step, but not the best example of lobbying. Voting for the congressperson is also just a first step to get him or her into office, and not part of the actual lobbying campaign.

50. D: Student sit-ins were an example in the 1960s of non-violent protesting that took place mostly under the guidance and philosophy of Martin Luther King, Jr. These were not displays of Black Power to incite fear, although those also occurred separately in the 1960s under leaders such as Malcolm X. Sit-ins were not a form of lobbying or litigation, although those are also non-violent in their nature.

51. D: Out of the four choices offered, the freedom of association or assembly BEST describes what constitutional right would be violated by the monitoring of religious or political groups, because people should be free to assemble and associate with whoever they wish without fear of government intervention. The other rights listed may have also been violated by the PATRIOT Act, but not in this particular example.

52. A: In this excerpt, de Tocqueville was discussing the American traits of egalitarianism ("citizens are drawn to the common level of an equal") and populism, or the interests and belief of the popular opinion ("common opinion" is powerful). The other choices all mention traits discussed by de Tocqueville in other parts of his book, but not in this particular excerpt.

53. A: The Sherman Antitrust Act of 1890 was the first law attempting to limit businesses that had monopolies. A student who understands that "trust" in this sense means a group of companies, and has come to mean "monopoly," may get the correct answer rather than choosing answer D, which uses a different meaning for the word "trust." It was not an attempt to limit businesses that were owned by foreigners or using child labor.

54. C: It is the best answer for the economic impact of the Homestead Act: Pioneers moved westward, built towns and schools, and created new states from former territories. The Act did cause a lot of westward settlement, unlike answer choice D, but it did not make agriculture the number one business in America, and it did not result in a political group called "Farmers for the Economy," even though those sound like answer choices that would be telling an economic impact of a law.

55. A: Although giving aid to poor people in Cuba does confer moral benefits for the donating country, making an argument for choice D, choice A is the BEST choice for the economic benefit to the U.S. of the Spanish-American War: the acquisition of island territories (such as Puerto Rico and the Philippines) that could provide new markets. Investing in Spain and the cost of repairing damaged ships would be economic negative costs of the war.

56. C: Raising taxes in the form of a War Revenue Act is the correct answer for this specific question of what was a third way to raise money that was used in 1917. The government may have cut some domestic spending, but not specifically in 1917 for this war. War bonds were sold to the public, but that is a method of borrowing money from the public, which was already mentioned as the first possible way to raise money for war. Choice A was not used in World War I; other governments did make purchases from the U.S. to help the war cause.

57. C: Speculation in the 1920s stock market helped cause the Great Depression. This is similar to speculation on the housing market in the 2000s causing today's recession, showing the student's mastery of skills in comparing and contrasting. Speculation on housing, high housing prices, and a 1920s recession were not causes of the Great Depression. The 1920s was a period of prosperity, not recession.

58. D: The kind of protectionism act by the U.S. that helped lead to a decline in worldwide trade, thus contributing to the Great Depression, was the raising of U.S. tariffs on imported goods. This led to other countries retaliating by raising tariffs also, so U.S. imports and exports were affected. Choice A and B were other causes of the Great Depression, but not

- 148 -

causes of the decline in worldwide trade directly. Choice C is the opposite of the correct answer.

59. D: A student will show that he or she can read a graph correctly and understand general social studies knowledge about the effects of the Great Depression if they choose D, "The Great Depression caused a steep increase in the rate of unemployment in the U.S." The rate was not originally high in 1929, but did steadily increase in the years following 1929. A student may think the graph shows the rate "steady" at one point, but it is still going up between 1932 and 1933. The unemployment rate of other countries is not shown on the graph, therefore making choice B incorrect.

60. B: While choices A and D may be partly responsible for some Mexican Americans leaving the U.S., several hundred thousand Mexican Americans were forcibly deported by the U.S. government (using troops to force them over the border) because of the Great Depression and lack of jobs in the U.S. So choice B is the correct answer as the main cause of the drop in the U.S.-Mexican population in the 1930s. Choice C was not really a factor in the drop.

61. D: "Rationing" was the name for this particular government program, and the reason for it was because food and other supplies were scarce and in greater demand during wartime. The G.I. Bill, Food Safety Act, and New Deal were all different kinds of government programs, some dealing with food but not all of them.

62. B: It best describes what all of the items on the list have in common. These were areas where women could find employment in non-traditional ways because of a manpower shortage during World War II. Women also worked outside the home in WWI, but Los Alamos and the baseball league were not set up that early. Choice D would be a good guess, but the All-American Girls Professional Baseball League was funded in the 1940s by businesses and businessmen, not by the federal government, unlike the other items on the list.

63. A: It is the best conclusion to be made based on the facts in the excerpt: Jobs for African Americans increased during World War II because of manpower needs and because of an anti-discrimination order from the president. The jobs would not have come without the executive order because there was still a lot of discrimination against African Americans in the 1940s (as is described in Coombs' book, paragraphs just before and after this excerpt). Roosevelt was concerned about Randolph planning a march because of how it might appear to U.S. enemies during the war, and Randolph was not bluffing. Randolph said discrimination by whites, not his march, was the reason that the U.S. would appear in a poor light to enemies or other countries.

64. B: The G.I. Bill, or Servicemen's Readjustment Act of 1944, was the name of the bill that had the myriad effects listed in the chart. The Taft-Hartley Act was an anti-labor bill under Truman; the Smith Act was a war time bill under FDR in 1940; and the Executive Order listed was one signed by Truman (although it would be a good guess because FDR did sign many "Executive Orders"). All the distracters are also near the same time period as the GI Bill, but students with a good general knowledge of history should get the correct answer.

65. A: Increased consumer spending and consumption can BEST be linked to the other three trends of the 1950s. An argument could be made that rock and roll music was also an

- *149* -

effect, but that cannot be tied directly to other three factors listed in the question, and it is a more specific and less general answer and therefore less correct answer for being in a cause/effect relationship with the other general trends. The military-industrial complex and Cold War were other trends in the 1950s, but they were not tied to the three trends mentioned in the question.

66. C: The GATT is now named the World Trade Organization, or WTO, and the U.S. is still a member. The student should know this from general social studies knowledge. If not, they might be able to rule out the ITA as a correct answer because "Administration" in the title gives a clue that the ITA is one country's (America's) internal organization, and not a worldwide organization.

67. B: The reason why laptop computers cost less today than in the early 1980s is that, because of the free enterprise system of the U.S., many companies now produce laptop computers and compete to sell them at lower costs. The government did not set price controls or take away any sales tax. Sales taxes vary from state to state. Choice D may be a true statement about how laptops have improved, but that option does not explain why the cost is less, and could even be used for an opposite argument for why laptops cost more to produce in modern times.

68. D: Statements A, B, and C all contain false statements about electric cars. Even if the student does not know enough about electric cars to determine that those statements are false, they probably would know enough to realize that statement D contains the best description of electric car advantages which contribute to a better standard of living for Americans using such cars: Electric cars have no tailpipe emissions, thus reducing air pollution in the U.S.; they lessen the country's dependence on foreign oil; and they are cheaper to operate than gas-powered cars.

Secret Key #1 - Time is Your Greatest Enemy

Pace Yourself

Wear a watch. At the beginning of the test, check the time (or start a chronometer on your watch to count the minutes), and check the time after every few questions to make sure you are "on schedule."

If you are forced to speed up, do it efficiently. Usually one or more answer choices can be eliminated without too much difficulty. Above all, don't panic. Don't speed up and just begin guessing at random choices. By pacing yourself, and continually monitoring your progress against your watch, you will always know exactly how far ahead or behind you are with your available time. If you find that you are one minute behind on the test, don't skip one question without spending any time on it, just to catch back up. Take 15 fewer seconds on the next four questions, and after four questions you'll have caught back up. Once you catch back up, you can continue working each problem at your normal pace.

Furthermore, don't dwell on the problems that you were rushed on. If a problem was taking up too much time and you made a hurried guess, it must be difficult. The difficult questions are the ones you are most likely to miss anyway, so it isn't a big loss. It is better to end with more time than you need than to run out of time.

Lastly, sometimes it is beneficial to slow down if you are constantly getting ahead of time. You are always more likely to catch a careless mistake by working more slowly than quickly, and among very high-scoring test takers (those who are likely to have lots of time left over), careless errors affect the score more than mastery of material.

Secret Key #2 - Guessing is not Guesswork

You probably know that guessing is a good idea. Unlike other standardized tests, there is no penalty for getting a wrong answer. Even if you have no idea about a question, you still have a 20-25% chance of getting it right.

Most test takers do not understand the impact that proper guessing can have on their score. Unless you score extremely high, guessing will significantly contribute to your final score.

Monkeys Take the Test

What most test takers don't realize is that to insure that 20-25% chance, you have to guess randomly. If you put 20 monkeys in a room to take this test, assuming they answered once per question and behaved themselves, on average they would get 20-25% of the questions correct. Put 20 test takers in the room, and the average will be much lower among guessed questions. Why?
  1. The test writers intentionally write deceptive answer choices that "look" right. A test

- 151 -

taker has no idea about a question, so he picks the "best looking" answer, which is often wrong. The monkey has no idea what looks good and what doesn't, so it will consistently be right about 20-25% of the time.

2. Test takers will eliminate answer choices from the guessing pool based on a hunch or intuition. Simple but correct answers often get excluded, leaving a 0% chance of being correct. The monkey has no clue, and often gets lucky with the best choice.

This is why the process of elimination endorsed by most test courses is flawed and detrimental to your performance. Test takers don't guess; they make an ignorant stab in the dark that is usually worse than random.

$5 Challenge

Let me introduce one of the most valuable ideas of this course—the $5 challenge:

You only mark your "best guess" if you are willing to bet $5 on it.
You only eliminate choices from guessing if you are willing to bet $5 on it.

Why $5? Five dollars is an amount of money that is small yet not insignificant, and can really add up fast (20 questions could cost you $100). Likewise, each answer choice on one question of the test will have a small impact on your overall score, but it can really add up to a lot of points in the end.

The process of elimination IS valuable. The following shows your chance of guessing it right:

If you eliminate wrong answer choices until only this many remain:	Chance of getting it correct:
1	100%
2	50%
3	33%

However, if you accidentally eliminate the right answer or go on a hunch for an incorrect answer, your chances drop dramatically—to 0%. By guessing among all the answer choices, you are GUARANTEED to have a shot at the right answer.

That's why the $5 test is so valuable. If you give up the advantage and safety of a pure guess, it had better be worth the risk.

What we still haven't covered is how to be sure that whatever guess you make is truly random. Here's the easiest way:

Always pick the first answer choice among those remaining.

Such a technique means that you have decided, **before you see a single test question**, exactly how you are going to guess, and since the order of choices tells you nothing about which one is correct, this guessing technique is perfectly random.

This section is not meant to scare you away from making educated guesses or eliminating choices; you just need to define when a choice is worth eliminating. The $5 test, along with a pre-defined random guessing strategy, is the best way to make sure you reap all of the benefits of guessing.

Secret Key #3 - Practice Smarter, Not Harder

Many test takers delay the test preparation process because they dread the awful amounts of practice time they think necessary to succeed on the test. We have refined an effective method that will take you only a fraction of the time.

There are a number of "obstacles" in the path to success. Among these are answering questions, finishing in time, and mastering test-taking strategies. All must be executed on the day of the test at peak performance, or your score will suffer. The test is a mental marathon that has a large impact on your future.

Just like a marathon runner, it is important to work your way up to the full challenge. So first you just worry about questions, and then time, and finally strategy:

Success Strategy

1. Find a good source for practice tests.
2. If you are willing to make a larger time investment, consider using more than one study guide. Often the different approaches of multiple authors will help you "get" difficult concepts.
3. Take a practice test with no time constraints, with all study helps, "open book." Take your time with questions and focus on applying strategies.
4. Take a practice test with time constraints, with all guides, "open book."
5. Take a final practice test without open material and with time limits.

If you have time to take more practice tests, just repeat step 5. By gradually exposing yourself to the full rigors of the test environment, you will condition your mind to the stress of test day and maximize your success.

Secret Key #4 - Prepare, Don't Procrastinate

Let me state an obvious fact: if you take the test three times, you will probably get three different scores. This is due to the way you feel on test day, the level of preparedness you have, and the version of the test you see. Despite the test writers' claims to the contrary, some versions of the test WILL be easier for you than others.

Since your future depends so much on your score, you should maximize your chances of success. In order to maximize the likelihood of success, you've got to prepare in advance. This means taking practice tests and spending time learning the information and test taking strategies you will need to succeed.

Never go take the actual test as a "practice" test, expecting that you can just take it again if you need to. Take all the practice tests you can on your own, but when you go to take the official test, be prepared, be focused, and do your best the first time!

Secret Key #5 - Test Yourself

Everyone knows that time is money. There is no need to spend too much of your time or too little of your time preparing for the test. You should only spend as much of your precious time preparing as is necessary for you to get the score you need.

Once you have taken a practice test under real conditions of time constraints, then you will know if you are ready for the test or not.

If you have scored extremely high the first time that you take the practice test, then there is not much point in spending countless hours studying. You are already there.

Benchmark your abilities by retaking practice tests and seeing how much you have improved. Once you consistently score high enough to guarantee success, then you are ready.

If you have scored well below where you need, then knuckle down and begin studying in earnest. Check your improvement regularly through the use of practice tests under real conditions. Above all, don't worry, panic, or give up. The key is perseverance!

Then, when you go to take the test, remain confident and remember how well you did on the practice tests. If you can score high enough on a practice test, then you can do the same on the real thing.

Success Strategies

The most important thing you can do is to ignore your fears and jump into the test immediately. Do not be overwhelmed by any strange-sounding terms. You have to jump into the test like jumping into a pool—all at once is the easiest way.

Make Predictions

As you read and understand the question, try to guess what the answer will be. Remember that several of the answer choices are wrong, and once you begin reading them, your mind will immediately become cluttered with answer choices designed to throw you off. Your mind is typically the most focused immediately after you have read the question and digested its contents. If you can, try to predict what the correct answer will be. You may be surprised at what you can predict.

Quickly scan the choices and see if your prediction is in the listed answer choices. If it is, then you can be quite confident that you have the right answer. It still won't hurt to check the other answer choices, but most of the time, you've got it!

Answer the Question

It may seem obvious to only pick answer choices that answer the question, but the test writers can create some excellent answer choices that are wrong. Don't pick an answer just because it sounds right, or you believe it to be true. It MUST answer the question. Once you've made your selection, always go back and check it against the question and make sure that you didn't misread the question and that the answer choice does answer the question posed.

Benchmark

After you read the first answer choice, decide if you think it sounds correct or not. If it doesn't, move on to the next answer choice. If it does, mentally mark that answer choice. This doesn't mean that you've definitely selected it as your answer choice, it just means that it's the best you've seen thus far. Go ahead and read the next choice. If the next choice is worse than the one you've already selected, keep going to the next answer choice. If the next choice is better than the choice you've already selected, mentally mark the new answer choice as your best guess.

The first answer choice that you select becomes your standard. Every other answer choice must be benchmarked against that standard. That choice is correct until proven otherwise by another answer choice beating it out. Once you've decided that no other answer choice seems as good, do one final check to ensure that your answer choice answers the question posed.

Valid Information

Don't discount any of the information provided in the question. Every piece of information may be necessary to determine the correct answer. None of the information in the question is there to throw you off (while the answer choices will certainly have information to throw you off). If two seemingly unrelated topics are discussed, don't ignore either. You can be confident there is a relationship, or it wouldn't be included in the question, and you are probably going to have to determine what is that relationship to find the answer.

Avoid "Fact Traps"

Don't get distracted by a choice that is factually true. Your search is for the answer that answers the question. Stay focused and don't fall for an answer that is true but irrelevant. Always go back to the question and make sure you're choosing an answer that actually answers the question and is not just a true statement. An answer can be factually correct, but it MUST answer the question asked. Additionally, two answers can both be seemingly correct, so be sure to read all of the answer choices, and make sure that you get the one that BEST answers the question.

Milk the Question

Some of the questions may throw you completely off. They might deal with a subject you have not been exposed to, or one that you haven't reviewed in years. While your lack of knowledge about the subject will be a hindrance, the question itself can give you many clues that will help you find the correct answer. Read the question carefully and look for clues. Watch particularly for adjectives and nouns describing difficult terms or words that you don't recognize. Regardless of whether you completely understand a word or not, replacing it with a synonym, either provided or one you more familiar with, may help you to understand what the questions are asking. Rather than wracking your mind about specific detailed information concerning a difficult term or word, try to use mental substitutes that are easier to understand.

The Trap of Familiarity

Don't just choose a word because you recognize it. On difficult questions, you may not recognize a number of words in the answer choices. The test writers don't put "make-believe" words on the test, so don't think that just because you only recognize all the words in one answer choice that that answer choice must be correct. If you only recognize words in one answer choice, then focus on that one. Is it correct? Try your best to determine if it is correct. If it is, that's great. If not, eliminate it. Each word and answer choice you eliminate increases your chances of getting the question correct, even if you then have to guess among the unfamiliar choices.

Eliminate Answers

Eliminate choices as soon as you realize they are wrong. But be careful! Make sure you consider all of the possible answer choices. Just because one appears right, doesn't mean that the next one won't be even better! The test writers will usually put more than one good answer choice for every question, so read all of them. Don't worry if you are stuck between two that seem right. By getting down to just two remaining possible choices, your odds are now 50/50. Rather than wasting too much time, play the odds. You are guessing, but guessing wisely because you've been able to knock out some of the answer choices that you know are wrong. If you are eliminating choices and realize that the last answer choice you are left with is also obviously wrong, don't panic. Start over and consider each choice again. There may easily be something that you missed the first time and will realize on the second pass.

Tough Questions

If you are stumped on a problem or it appears too hard or too difficult, don't waste time. Move on! Remember though, if you can quickly check for obviously incorrect answer choices, your chances of guessing correctly are greatly improved. Before you completely give up, at least try to knock out a couple of possible answers. Eliminate what you can and then guess at the remaining answer choices before moving on.

Brainstorm

If you get stuck on a difficult question, spend a few seconds quickly brainstorming. Run through the complete list of possible answer choices. Look at each choice and ask yourself, "Could this answer the question satisfactorily?" Go through each answer choice and consider it independently of the others. By systematically going through all possibilities, you may find something that you would otherwise overlook. Remember though that when you get stuck, it's important to try to keep moving.

Read Carefully

Understand the problem. Read the question and answer choices carefully. Don't miss the question because you misread the terms. You have plenty of time to read each question thoroughly and make sure you understand what is being asked. Yet a happy medium must be attained, so don't waste too much time. You must read carefully, but efficiently.

Face Value

When in doubt, use common sense. Always accept the situation in the problem at face value. Don't read too much into it. These problems will not require you to make huge leaps of logic. The test writers aren't trying to throw you off with a cheap trick. If you have to go beyond creativity and make a leap of logic in order to have an answer choice answer the question, then you should look at the other answer choices. Don't overcomplicate the problem by creating theoretical relationships or explanations that will warp time or space. These are normal problems rooted in reality. It's just that the applicable relationship or explanation may not be readily apparent and you have to figure things out. Use your common sense to interpret anything that isn't clear.

Prefixes

If you're having trouble with a word in the question or answer choices, try dissecting it. Take advantage of every clue that the word might include. Prefixes and suffixes can be a huge help. Usually they allow you to determine a basic meaning. Pre- means before, post- means after, pro - is positive, de- is negative. From these prefixes and suffixes, you can get an idea of the general meaning of the word and try to put it into context. Beware though of any traps. Just because con- is the opposite of pro-, doesn't necessarily mean congress is the opposite of progress!

Hedge Phrases

Watch out for critical hedge phrases, led off with words such as "likely," "may," "can," "sometimes," "often," "almost," "mostly," "usually," "generally," "rarely," and "sometimes." Question writers insert these hedge phrases to cover every possibility. Often an answer choice will be wrong simply because it leaves no room for exception. Unless the situation calls for them, avoid answer choices that have definitive words like "exactly," and "always."

Switchback Words

Stay alert for "switchbacks." These are the words and phrases frequently used to alert you to shifts in thought. The most common switchback word is "but." Others include "although," "however," "nevertheless," "on the other hand," "even though," "while," "in spite of," "despite," and "regardless of."

New Information

Correct answer choices will rarely have completely new information included. Answer choices typically are straightforward reflections of the material asked about and will directly relate to the question. If a new piece of information is included in an answer choice that doesn't even seem to relate to the topic being asked about, then that answer choice is likely incorrect. All of the information needed to answer the question is usually provided for you in the question. You should not have to make guesses that are unsupported or choose answer choices that require unknown information that cannot be reasoned from what is given.

Time Management

On technical questions, don't get lost on the technical terms. Don't spend too much time on any one question. If you don't know what a term means, then odds are you aren't going to get much further since you don't have a dictionary. You should be able to immediately recognize whether or not you know a term. If you don't, work with the other clues that you have—the other answer choices and terms provided—but don't waste too much time trying to figure out a difficult term that you don't know.

Contextual Clues

Look for contextual clues. An answer can be right but not the correct answer. The contextual clues will help you find the answer that is most right and is correct. Understand the context in which a phrase or statement is made. This will help you make important distinctions.

Don't Panic

Panicking will not answer any questions for you; therefore, it isn't helpful. When you first see the question, if your mind goes blank, take a deep breath. Force yourself to mechanically go through the steps of solving the problem using the strategies you've learned.

Pace Yourself

Don't get clock fever. It's easy to be overwhelmed when you're looking at a page full of questions, your mind is full of random thoughts and feeling confused, and the clock is ticking down faster than you would like. Calm down and maintain the pace that you have set for yourself. As long as you are on track by monitoring your pace, you are guaranteed to have enough time for yourself. When you get to the last few minutes of the test, it may seem like you won't have enough time left, but if you only have as many questions as you should have left at that point, then you're right on track!

Answer Selection

The best way to pick an answer choice is to eliminate all of those that are wrong, until only one is left and confirm that is the correct answer. Sometimes though, an answer choice may immediately look right. Be careful! Take a second to make sure that the other choices are not equally obvious. Don't make a hasty mistake. There are only two times that you should stop before checking other answers. First is when you are positive that the answer choice you have selected is correct. Second is when time is almost out and you have to make a quick guess!

Check Your Work

Since you will probably not know every term listed and the answer to every question, it is important that you get credit for the ones that you do know. Don't miss any questions through careless mistakes. If at all possible, try to take a second to look back over your answer selection and make sure you've selected the correct answer choice and haven't made a costly careless mistake (such as marking an answer choice that you didn't mean to mark). The time it takes for this quick double check should more than pay for itself in caught mistakes.

Beware of Directly Quoted Answers

Sometimes an answer choice will repeat word for word a portion of the question or reference section. However, beware of such exact duplication. It may be a trap! More than likely, the correct choice will paraphrase or summarize a point, rather than being exactly the same wording.

Slang

Scientific sounding answers are better than slang ones. An answer choice that begins "To compare the outcomes..." is much more likely to be correct than one that begins "Because some people insisted..."

Extreme Statements

Avoid wild answers that throw out highly controversial ideas that are proclaimed as established fact. An answer choice that states the "process should used in certain situations, if..." is much more likely to be correct than one that states the "process should be discontinued completely." The first is a calm rational statement and doesn't even make a definitive, uncompromising stance, using a hedge word "if" to provide wiggle room, whereas the second choice is a radical idea and far more extreme.

Answer Choice Families

When you have two or more answer choices that are direct opposites or parallels, one of them is usually the correct answer. For instance, if one answer choice states "x increases" and another answer choice states "x decreases" or "y increases," then those two or three answer choices are very similar in construction and fall into the same family of answer choices. A family of answer choices consists of two or three answer choices, very similar in construction, but often with directly opposite meanings. Usually the correct answer choice will be in that family of answer choices. The "odd man out" or answer choice that doesn't seem to fit the parallel construction of the other answer choices is more likely to be incorrect.

Special Report: How to Overcome Test Anxiety

The very nature of tests caters to some level of anxiety, nervousness, or tension, just as we feel for any important event that occurs in our lives. A little bit of anxiety or nervousness can be a good thing. It helps us with motivation, and makes achievement just that much sweeter. However, too much anxiety can be a problem, especially if it hinders our ability to function and perform.

"Test anxiety," is the term that refers to the emotional reactions that some test-takers experience when faced with a test or exam. Having a fear of testing and exams is based upon a rational fear, since the test-taker's performance can shape the course of an academic career. Nevertheless, experiencing excessive fear of examinations will only interfere with the test-taker's ability to perform and chance to be successful.

There are a large variety of causes that can contribute to the development and sensation of test anxiety. These include, but are not limited to, lack of preparation and worrying about issues surrounding the test.

Lack of Preparation

Lack of preparation can be identified by the following behaviors or situations:

Not scheduling enough time to study, and therefore cramming the night before the test or exam
Managing time poorly, to create the sensation that there is not enough time to do everything
Failing to organize the text information in advance, so that the study material consists of the entire text and not simply the pertinent information
Poor overall studying habits

Worrying, on the other hand, can be related to both the test taker, or many other factors around him/her that will be affected by the results of the test. These include worrying about:

Previous performances on similar exams, or exams in general
How friends and other students are achieving
The negative consequences that will result from a poor grade or failure

There are three primary elements to test anxiety. Physical components, which involve the same typical bodily reactions as those to acute anxiety (to be discussed below). Emotional factors have to do with fear or panic. Mental or cognitive issues concerning attention spans and memory abilities.

Physical Signals

There are many different symptoms of test anxiety, and these are not limited to mental and emotional strain. Frequently there are a range of physical signals that will let a test taker know that he/she is suffering from test anxiety. These bodily changes can include the following:

Perspiring
Sweaty palms
Wet, trembling hands
Nausea
Dry mouth
A knot in the stomach
Headache
Faintness
Muscle tension
Aching shoulders, back and neck
Rapid heart beat
Feeling too hot/cold

To recognize the sensation of test anxiety, a test-taker should monitor him/herself for the following sensations:

The physical distress symptoms as listed above
Emotional sensitivity, expressing emotional feelings such as the need to cry or laugh too much, or a sensation of anger or helplessness
A decreased ability to think, causing the test-taker to blank out or have racing thoughts that are hard to organize or control.

Though most students will feel some level of anxiety when faced with a test or exam, the majority can cope with that anxiety and maintain it at a manageable level. However, those who cannot are faced with a very real and very serious condition, which can and should be controlled for the immeasurable benefit of this sufferer.

Naturally, these sensations lead to negative results for the testing experience. The most common effects of test anxiety have to do with nervousness and mental blocking.

Nervousness

Nervousness can appear in several different levels:

The test-taker's difficulty, or even inability to read and understand the questions on the test
The difficulty or inability to organize thoughts to a coherent form
The difficulty or inability to recall key words and concepts relating to the testing questions (especially essays)
The receipt of poor grades on a test, though the test material was well known by the test taker

Conversely, a person may also experience mental blocking, which involves:

Blanking out on test questions
Only remembering the correct answers to the questions when the test has already finished.

Fortunately for test anxiety sufferers, beating these feelings, to a large degree, has to do with proper preparation. When a test taker has a feeling of preparedness, then anxiety will be dramatically lessened.

The first step to resolving anxiety issues is to distinguish which of the two types of anxiety are being suffered. If the anxiety is a direct result of a lack of preparation, this should be considered a normal reaction, and the anxiety level (as opposed to the test results) shouldn't be anything to worry about. However, if, when adequately prepared, the test-taker still panics, blanks out, or seems to overreact, this is not a fully rational reaction. While this can be considered normal too, there are many ways to combat and overcome these effects.

Remember that anxiety cannot be entirely eliminated, however, there are ways to minimize it, to make the anxiety easier to manage. Preparation is one of the best ways to minimize test anxiety. Therefore the following techniques are wise in order to best fight off any anxiety that may want to build.

To begin with, try to avoid cramming before a test, whenever it is possible. By trying to memorize an entire term's worth of information in one day, you'll be shocking your system, and not giving yourself a very good chance to absorb the information. This is an easy path to anxiety, so for those who suffer from test anxiety, cramming should not even be considered an option.

Instead of cramming, work throughout the semester to combine all of the material which is presented throughout the semester, and work on it gradually as the course goes by, making sure to master the main concepts first, leaving minor details for a week or so before the test.

To study for the upcoming exam, be sure to pose questions that may be on the examination, to gauge the ability to answer them by integrating the ideas from your texts, notes and lectures, as well as any supplementary readings.

If it is truly impossible to cover all of the information that was covered in that particular term, concentrate on the most important portions, that can be covered very well. Learn these concepts as best as possible, so that when the test comes, a goal can be made to use these concepts as presentations of your knowledge.

In addition to study habits, changes in attitude are critical to beating a struggle with test anxiety. In fact, an improvement of the perspective over the entire test-taking experience can actually help a test taker to enjoy studying and therefore improve the overall experience. Be certain not to overemphasize the significance of the grade - know that the result of the test is neither a reflection of self worth, nor is it a measure of intelligence; one grade will not predict a person's future success.

To improve an overall testing outlook, the following steps should be tried:

Keeping in mind that the most reasonable expectation for taking a test is to expect to try to demonstrate as much of what you know as you possibly can.
Reminding ourselves that a test is only one test; this is not the only one, and there will be others.
The thought of thinking of oneself in an irrational, all-or-nothing term should be avoided at all costs.
A reward should be designated for after the test, so there's something to look forward to. Whether it be going to a movie, going out to eat, or simply visiting friends, schedule it in advance, and do it no matter what result is expected on the exam.

Test-takers should also keep in mind that the basics are some of the most important things, even beyond anti-anxiety techniques and studying. Never neglect the basic social, emotional and biological needs, in order to try to absorb information. In order to best achieve, these three factors must be held as just as important as the studying itself.

Study Steps

Remember the following important steps for studying:

Maintain healthy nutrition and exercise habits. Continue both your recreational activities and social pass times. These both contribute to your physical and emotional well being.
Be certain to get a good amount of sleep, especially the night before the test, because when you're overtired you are not able to perform to the best of your best ability.
Keep the studying pace to a moderate level by taking breaks when they are needed, and varying the work whenever possible, to keep the mind fresh instead of getting bored. When enough studying has been done that all the material that can be learned has been learned, and the test taker is prepared for the test, stop studying and do something relaxing such as listening to music, watching a movie, or taking a warm bubble bath.

There are also many other techniques to minimize the uneasiness or apprehension that is experienced along with test anxiety before, during, or even after the examination. In fact, there are a great deal of things that can be done to stop anxiety from interfering with lifestyle and performance. Again, remember that anxiety will not be eliminated entirely, and it shouldn't be. Otherwise that "up" feeling for exams would not exist, and most of us depend on that sensation to perform better than usual. However, this anxiety has to be at a level that is manageable.

Of course, as we have just discussed, being prepared for the exam is half the battle right away. Attending all classes, finding out what knowledge will be expected on the exam, and knowing the exam schedules are easy steps to lowering anxiety. Keeping up with work will remove the need to cram, and efficient study habits will eliminate wasted time. Studying should be done in an ideal location for concentration, so that it is simple to become interested in the material and give it complete attention. A method such as SQ3R (Survey, Question, Read, Recite, Review) is a wonderful key to follow to make sure that the study habits are as effective as possible, especially in the case of learning from a textbook. Flashcards are great techniques for memorization. Learning to take good notes will mean that notes will be full of useful information, so that less sifting will need to be done to seek out what is pertinent for studying. Reviewing notes after class and then again on occasion will keep the information fresh in the mind. From notes that have been taken summary sheets and outlines can be made for simpler reviewing.

A study group can also be a very motivational and helpful place to study, as there will be a sharing of ideas, all of the minds can work together, to make sure that everyone understands, and the studying will be made more interesting because it will be a social occasion.

Basically, though, as long as the test-taker remains organized and self confident, with efficient study habits, less time will need to be spent studying, and higher grades will be achieved.

To become self confident, there are many useful steps. The first of these is "self talk." It has been shown through extensive research, that self-talk for students who suffer from test anxiety, should be well monitored, in order to make sure that it contributes to self confidence as opposed to sinking the student. Frequently the self talk of test-anxious students is negative or self-defeating, thinking that everyone else is smarter and faster, that they always mess up, and that if they don't do well, they'll fail the entire course. It is important to decreasing anxiety that awareness is made of self talk. Try writing any negative self thoughts and then disputing them with a positive statement instead. Begin self-encouragement as though it was a friend speaking. Repeat positive statements to help reprogram the mind to believing in successes instead of failures.

Helpful Techniques

Other extremely helpful techniques include:

Self-visualization of doing well and reaching goals
While aiming for an "A" level of understanding, don't try to "overprotect" by setting your expectations lower. This will only convince the mind to stop studying in order to meet the lower expectations.
Don't make comparisons with the results or habits of other students. These are individual factors, and different things work for different people, causing different results.
Strive to become an expert in learning what works well, and what can be done in order to improve. Consider collecting this data in a journal.
Create rewards for after studying instead of doing things before studying that will only turn into avoidance behaviors.
Make a practice of relaxing - by using methods such as progressive relaxation, self-hypnosis, guided imagery, etc - in order to make relaxation an automatic sensation.
Work on creating a state of relaxed concentration so that concentrating will take on the focus of the mind, so that none will be wasted on worrying.
Take good care of the physical self by eating well and getting enough sleep.
Plan in time for exercise and stick to this plan.

Beyond these techniques, there are other methods to be used before, during and after the test that will help the test-taker perform well in addition to overcoming anxiety.

Before the exam comes the academic preparation. This involves establishing a study schedule and beginning at least one week before the actual date of the test. By doing this, the anxiety of not having enough time to study for the test will be automatically eliminated. Moreover, this will make the studying a much more effective experience, ensuring that the learning will be an easier process. This relieves much undue pressure on the test-taker.

Summary sheets, note cards, and flash cards with the main concepts and examples of these main concepts should be prepared in advance of the actual studying time. A topic should never be eliminated from this process. By omitting a topic because it isn't expected to be on the test is only setting up the test-taker for anxiety should it actually appear on the exam. Utilize the course syllabus for laying out the topics that should be studied. Carefully go over the notes that were made in class, paying special attention to any of the issues that the professor took special care to emphasize while lecturing in class. In the textbooks, use the chapter review, or if possible, the chapter tests, to begin your review.

It may even be possible to ask the instructor what information will be covered on the exam, or what the format of the exam will be (for example, multiple choice, essay, free form, true-false). Additionally, see if it is possible to find out how many questions will be on the test. If a review sheet or sample test has been offered by the professor, make good use of it, above anything else, for the preparation for the test. Another great resource for getting to know the examination is reviewing tests from previous semesters. Use these tests to review, and aim to achieve a 100% score on each of the possible topics. With a few exceptions, the goal that you set for yourself is the highest one that you will reach.

Take all of the questions that were assigned as homework, and rework them to any other possible course material. The more problems reworked, the more skill and confidence will form as a result. When forming the solution to a problem, write out each of the steps. Don't simply do head work. By doing as many steps on paper as possible, much clarification and therefore confidence will be formed. Do this with as many homework problems as possible, before checking the answers. By checking the answer after each problem, a reinforcement will exist, that will not be on the exam. Study situations should be as exam-like as possible, to prime the test-taker's system for the experience. By waiting to check the answers at the end, a psychological advantage will be formed, to decrease the stress factor.

Another fantastic reason for not cramming is the avoidance of confusion in concepts, especially when it comes to mathematics. 8-10 hours of study will become one hundred percent more effective if it is spread out over a week or at least several days, instead of doing it all in one sitting. Recognize that the human brain requires time in order to assimilate new material, so frequent breaks and a span of study time over several days will be much more beneficial.

Additionally, don't study right up until the point of the exam. Studying should stop a minimum of one hour before the exam begins. This allows the brain to rest and put things in their proper order. This will also provide the time to become as relaxed as possible when going into the examination room. The test-taker will also have time to eat well and eat sensibly. Know that the brain needs food as much as the rest of the body. With enough food and enough sleep, as well as a relaxed attitude, the body and the mind are primed for success.

Avoid any anxious classmates who are talking about the exam. These students only spread anxiety, and are not worth sharing the anxious sentimentalities.

Before the test also involves creating a positive attitude, so mental preparation should also be a point of concentration. There are many keys to creating a positive attitude. Should fears become rushing in, make a visualization of taking the exam, doing well, and seeing an A written on the paper. Write out a list of affirmations that will bring a feeling of confidence, such as "I am doing well in my English class," "I studied well and know my material," "I enjoy this class." Even if the affirmations aren't believed at first, it sends a positive message to the subconscious which will result in an alteration of the overall belief system, which is the system that creates reality.

If a sensation of panic begins, work with the fear and imagine the very worst! Work through the entire scenario of not passing the test, failing the entire course, and dropping out of school, followed by not getting a job, and pushing a shopping cart through the dark alley where you'll live. This will place things into perspective! Then, practice deep breathing and create a visualization of the opposite situation - achieving an "A" on the exam, passing the entire course, receiving the degree at a graduation ceremony.

On the day of the test, there are many things to be done to ensure the best results, as well as the most calm outlook. The following stages are suggested in order to maximize test-taking potential:

Begin the examination day with a moderate breakfast, and avoid any coffee or beverages with caffeine if the test taker is prone to jitters. Even people who are used to managing caffeine can feel jittery or light-headed when it is taken on a test day. Attempt to do something that is relaxing before the examination begins. As last minute cramming clouds the mastering of overall concepts, it is better to use this time to create a calming outlook.
Be certain to arrive at the test location well in advance, in order to provide time to select a location that is away from doors, windows and other distractions, as well as giving enough time to relax before the test begins.
Keep away from anxiety generating classmates who will upset the sensation of stability and relaxation that is being attempted before the exam.
Should the waiting period before the exam begins cause anxiety, create a self-distraction by reading a light magazine or something else that is relaxing and simple.

During the exam itself, read the entire exam from beginning to end, and find out how much time should be allotted to each individual problem. Once writing the exam, should more time be taken for a problem, it should be abandoned, in order to begin

- 166 -

another problem. If there is time at the end, the unfinished problem can always be returned to and completed.

Read the instructions very carefully - twice - so that unpleasant surprises won't follow during or after the exam has ended.

When writing the exam, pretend that the situation is actually simply the completion of homework within a library, or at home. This will assist in forming a relaxed atmosphere, and will allow the brain extra focus for the complex thinking function.

Begin the exam with all of the questions with which the most confidence is felt. This will build the confidence level regarding the entire exam and will begin a quality momentum. This will also create encouragement for trying the problems where uncertainty resides.

Going with the "gut instinct" is always the way to go when solving a problem. Second guessing should be avoided at all costs. Have confidence in the ability to do well.

For essay questions, create an outline in advance that will keep the mind organized and make certain that all of the points are remembered. For multiple choice, read every answer, even if the correct one has been spotted - a better one may exist.

Continue at a pace that is reasonable and not rushed, in order to be able to work carefully. Provide enough time to go over the answers at the end, to check for small errors that can be corrected.

Should a feeling of panic begin, breathe deeply, and think of the feeling of the body releasing sand through its pores. Visualize a calm, peaceful place, and include all of the sights, sounds and sensations of this image. Continue the deep breathing, and take a few minutes to continue this with closed eyes. When all is well again, return to the test.

If a "blanking" occurs for a certain question, skip it and move on to the next question. There will be time to return to the other question later. Get everything done that can be done, first, to guarantee all the grades that can be compiled, and to build all of the confidence possible. Then return to the weaker questions to build the marks from there.

Remember, one's own reality can be created, so as long as the belief is there, success will follow. And remember: anxiety can happen later, right now, there's an exam to be written!

After the examination is complete, whether there is a feeling for a good grade or a bad grade, don't dwell on the exam, and be certain to follow through on the reward that was promised...and enjoy it! Don't dwell on any mistakes that have been made, as there is nothing that can be done at this point anyway.

Additionally, don't begin to study for the next test right away. Do something relaxing for a while, and let the mind relax and prepare itself to begin absorbing information again.

From the results of the exam - both the grade and the entire experience, be certain to learn from what has gone on. Perfect studying habits and work some more on confidence in order to make the next examination experience even better than the last one.

Learn to avoid places where openings occurred for laziness, procrastination and day dreaming.

Use the time between this exam and the next one to better learn to relax, even learning to relax on cue, so that any anxiety can be controlled during the next exam. Learn how to relax the body. Slouch in your chair if that helps. Tighten and then relax all of the different muscle groups, one group at a time, beginning with the feet and then working all the way up to the neck and face. This will ultimately relax the muscles more than they were to begin with. Learn how to breathe deeply and comfortably, and focus on this breathing going in and out as a relaxing thought. With every exhale, repeat the word "relax."

As common as test anxiety is, it is very possible to overcome it. Make yourself one of the test-takers who overcome this frustrating hindrance.

Additional Bonus Material

Due to our efforts to try to keep this book to a manageable length, we've created a link that will give you access to all of your additional bonus material.

Please visit http://www.mometrix.com/bonus948/gaushistory to access the information.

R0170387350